OPPOSING VIEWPOINTS® SERIES

Voting Rights

Other Books of Related Interest

Opposing Viewpoints Series
Government Spending
Nation Building
The Presidential Election Process

Current Controversies Series
Developing Nations
Domestic Wiretapping

At Issue Series
Political Activism
Should the United States Move to Electronic Voting?
Should the Voting Age Be Lowered?

"Congress shall make no law . . . abridging the freedom of speech, or of the press."

First Amendment to the U.S. Constitution

The basic foundation of our democracy is the First Amendment guarantee of freedom of expression. The Opposing Viewpoints Series is dedicated to the concept of this basic freedom and the idea that it is more important to practice it than to enshrine it.

OPPOSING VIEWPOINTS® SERIES

Voting Rights

Tom Lansford, Book Editor

GREENHAVEN PRESS
A part of Gale, Cengage Learning

GALE
CENGAGE Learning™

Detroit • New York • San Francisco • New Haven, Conn • Waterville, Maine • London

Christine Nasso, *Publisher*
Elizabeth Des Chenes, *Managing Editor*

© 2008 Greenhaven Press, a part of Gale, Cengage Learning.

Gale and Greenhaven Press are registered trademarks used herein under license.

For more information, contact:
Greenhaven Press
27500 Drake Rd.
Farmington Hills, MI 48331-3535
Or you can visit our Internet site at gale.cengage.com

For product information and technology assistance, contact us at

Gale Customer Support, 1-800-877-4253
For permission to use material from this text or product, submit all requests online at
www.cengage.com/permissions

Further permissions questions can be emailed to permissionrequest@cengage.com

Articles in Greenhaven Press anthologies are often edited for length to meet page requirements. In addition, original titles of these works are changed to clearly present the main thesis and to explicitly indicate the author's opinion. Every effort is made to ensure that Greenhaven Press accurately reflects the original intent of the authors. Every effort has been made to trace the owners of copyrighted material.

Cover photograph reproduced by permission of David Silverman/Getty Images News/Getty Images.

LIBRARY OF CONGRESS CATALOGING-IN-PUBLICATION DATA

Voting rights / Tom Lansford, book editor.
  p. cm. -- (Opposing viewpoints)
  Includes bibliographical references and index.
  ISBN-13: 978-0-7377-4014-1 (hardcover)
  ISBN-13: 978-0-7377-4015-8 (pbk.)
  1. Voting. I. Lansford, Tom.
  JF1001.V69 2008
  324.6'2--dc22

                                                     2008012800

Printed in the United States of America
2 3 4 5 6   13 12 11 10 09

Contents

Why Consider
Opposing Viewpoints?

"The only way in which a human being can make some approach to knowing the whole of a subject is by hearing what can be said about it by persons of every variety of opinion and studying all modes in which it can be looked at by every character of mind. No wise man ever acquired his wisdom in any mode but this."

John Stuart Mill

In our media-intensive culture it is not difficult to find differing opinions. Thousands of newspapers and magazines and dozens of radio and television talk shows resound with differing points of view. The difficulty lies in deciding which opinion to agree with and which "experts" seem the most credible. The more inundated we become with differing opinions and claims, the more essential it is to hone critical reading and thinking skills to evaluate these ideas. Opposing Viewpoints books address this problem directly by presenting stimulating debates that can be used to enhance and teach these skills. The varied opinions contained in each book examine many different aspects of a single issue. While examining these conveniently edited opposing views, readers can develop critical thinking skills such as the ability to compare and contrast authors' credibility, facts, argumentation styles, use of persuasive techniques, and other stylistic tools. In short, the Opposing Viewpoints Series is an ideal way to attain the higher-level thinking and reading skills so essential in a culture of diverse and contradictory opinions.

In addition to providing a tool for critical thinking, Opposing Viewpoints books challenge readers to question their own strongly held opinions and assumptions. Most people form their opinions on the basis of upbringing, peer pressure, and personal, cultural, or professional bias. By reading carefully balanced opposing views, readers must directly confront new ideas as well as the opinions of those with whom they disagree. This is not to simplistically argue that everyone who reads opposing views will—or should—change his or her opinion. Instead, the series enhances readers' understanding of their own views by encouraging confrontation with opposing ideas. Careful examination of others' views can lead to the readers' understanding of the logical inconsistencies in their own opinions, perspective on why they hold an opinion, and the consideration of the possibility that their opinion requires further evaluation.

Evaluating Other Opinions

To ensure that this type of examination occurs, Opposing Viewpoints books present all types of opinions. Prominent spokespeople on different sides of each issue as well as well-known professionals from many disciplines challenge the reader. An additional goal of the series is to provide a forum for other, less known, or even unpopular viewpoints. The opinion of an ordinary person who has had to make the decision to cut off life support from a terminally ill relative, for example, may be just as valuable and provide just as much insight as a medical ethicist's professional opinion. The editors have two additional purposes in including these less known views. One, the editors encourage readers to respect others' opinions—even when not enhanced by professional credibility. It is only by reading or listening to and objectively evaluating others' ideas that one can determine whether they are worthy of consideration. Two, the inclusion of such viewpoints encourages the important critical thinking skill of objectively evaluating an author's credentials and bias. This evaluation will illuminate an author's reasons for taking a particular stance on an issue and will aid in readers' evaluation of the author's ideas.

It is our hope that these books will give readers a deeper understanding of the issues debated and an appreciation of the complexity of even seemingly simple issues when good and honest people disagree. This awareness is particularly important in a democratic society such as ours in which people enter into public debate to determine the common good. Those with whom one disagrees should not be regarded as enemies but rather as people whose views deserve careful examination and may shed light on one's own.

Thomas Jefferson once said that "difference of opinion leads to inquiry, and inquiry to truth." Jefferson, a broadly educated man, argued that "if a nation expects to be ignorant and free . . . it expects what never was and never will be." As individuals and as a nation, it is imperative that we consider the opinions of others and examine them with skill and discernment. The Opposing Viewpoints Series is intended to help readers achieve this goal.

David L. Bender and Bruno Leone,
Founders

Introduction

> "It doesn't matter how heinous the crime; everyone is entitled to have the basic human right to vote."
>
> John Hirst

On February 11, 1980, John Hirst, a British citizen, pleaded guilty to manslaughter charges for a crime in which he killed Bronia Burton, his sixty-two-year-old landlady, with an axe. Hirst was judged at the time to have a violent personality disorder. He was sentenced to life in prison, with the potential for parole. When he entered prison, Hirst attempted to register to vote, but his application was denied. The United Kingdom had passed a law in 1870 that forbade anyone serving time in prison from voting. The law had been amended several times, most recently in the 1983 Representation of the People Act, when its wording was revised to read: "A convicted person during the time that he is detained in a penal institution . . . is legally incapable of voting at any parliamentary or local government election."

In 2001, Hirst and two other convicts sued the British government claiming that their political rights were being infringed by the prohibition on prisoner voting. Their case went all the way to the British High Court, which ultimately rejected their assertions and ruled that it was within the rights of the government to restrict voting privileges because of criminal behavior. Hirst refused to accept the ruling and appealed to the European Court of Human Rights, which oversees the domestic laws of the United Kingdom and other signatories of the 1950 European Convention on Human Rights. While the court was considering his case, Hirst was released from prison on parole. In March 2004, the European Court ruled in his favor, declaring that voting was integral to modern democracy and that participating in elections was an important step in rehabilitating criminals. Peter Benchley, a leading British politician, endorsed the decision and spoke of the practical impact: "Voting in prison can be a useful first step to engaging in society."

The court did rule, however, that governments had the right to disenfranchise, or take away the voting rights of, convicted criminals if they had committed crimes against the state. In other words, people convicted of treason, political corruption, or other offenses against the government could lose their right to vote for specific periods of time. By court order, people with certain mental disabilities could also be barred from voting. After the ruling, Hirst explained why he went to court: "Every human being has rights and it is up to us all to ensure that those people get those human rights and not say 'oh because they're a prisoner they should be denied them.'"

Hirst was awarded sixteen thousand British pounds (nearly twenty-eight thousand U.S. dollars) in compensation for the loss of his voting rights while he was in prison. The ruling was upheld when the British government appealed the decision to the European Court of Justice. According to the ruling, forty-eight thousand prisoners in the United Kingdom were to be given the right to vote and British officials were ordered to allow people to vote while incarcerated. In addition, the forty-six countries that had signed the European Convention on Human Rights were ordered to begin removing restrictions on convict voting.

Many in the United Kingdom protested the ruling. Dominic Grieve, a conservative politician, declared that the decision would "bring the law into disrepute and many people will see it as making a mockery of justice." Victims' rights groups condemned the case and contended that those who violated the law should be subject to the loss of many of their civil and political rights. Some Britons argued that the loss of voting rights was a legitimate punishment for committing crimes against society. Others contended that it was not fair that criminals would be able to vote and therefore influence national decisions on matters such as crime, law enforcement, and punishment policy. In the face of public pressure, the British government has banned voting by prisoners, despite the rulings of the European courts.

A number of countries, including the United States, have similar measures that restrict prisoners or convicts from voting. Armenia, Bulgaria, the Czech Republic, Estonia, Hungary, Luxembourg, Romania, and Russia automatically disenfranchise prisoners once they are convicted of a crime. The concept is known as "civic death" and it means that the government has the right to take away the civil rights and liberties of people who have transgressed against society. The principle exists to a lesser degree in other forms of punishment. For instance, people put in prison lose their freedom of movement while individuals who violate traffic regulations can lose the privilege to drive a car.

Policies that disenfranchise people convicted of crimes vary from country to country. For instance, in several countries, prisoners who are serving sentences of five years or longer, or who have committed certain crimes against the state, are not allowed to vote, but those serving lesser sentences can cast ballots even though they are in jail. In France and Germany, a judge can disenfranchise a convict, depending upon the crime and prison sentence. In the United States, the individual states decide whether or not prisoners lose their right to vote. Maine and Vermont do not disenfranchise prisoners, but the other forty-eight states bar convicts from voting while they are in prison. Thirty-seven states and the District of Columbia automatically restore voting rights after prisoners complete their sentence (including parole and probation in some cases). Alabama, Florida, Kentucky, and Virginia ban people convicted of felonies from voting for life, although individuals can petition to have their rights restored under certain circumstances.

Other countries have removed the restrictions on prisoner voting. For example, South Africa ended prisoner disenfranchisement in 1999. In Canada in 2002, the Supreme Court, in the case *Sauvé v. Canada*, ruled that prisoners should have the ability to cast ballots. In issuing its ruling, the court declared that "to deny prisoners the right to vote is to lose an important means of teaching them democratic values and social responsibility." Subsequently, prisoners voted for the first time in Canada in the 2004 elections. In August 2007, the Australian Supreme Court ruled that the country's prohibition on prisoner voting was unconstitutional and the government had to revise its laws.

Around the world, prisoners are but one group whose voting rights are often infringed on. Women, expatriates, and minors are others. Proponents of expanding voting rights argue that voting is such an important part of democracy that all people should be allowed to cast ballots. While opponents contend that voting is a privilege that should be earned through citizenship and adherence to the law. The authors in *Opposing Viewpoints: Voting Rights* examine voting rights controversies in the following chapters: Should Everyone Be Allowed to Vote? Should Voting Be Mandatory? Should Voting Rights for Women Be Expanded? and How Should Global Voting Rights Be Expanded? No doubt, the debate over voting rights will continue to play a central role in the development of democracy across the globe.

OPPOSING
VIEWPOINTS®
SERIES

CHAPTER 1

Should Everyone Be Allowed to Vote?

Chapter Preface

Voting is a political right enjoyed by a country's citizens. However, in some instances, a person's voting rights may be taken away temporarily or even permanently. For instance, most countries do not allow people convicted of certain serious crimes to vote. In the United States, the individual fifty states set their own laws on voting. Two states, Maine and Vermont, have no restrictions to prevent convicts from voting, while other states allow convicts who have served their sentence to petition to have their voting rights restored. Alabama, Florida, Kentucky, and Virginia do not allow felons to vote even after they are released from prison. Many people argue that once convicts have paid their debt to society, their voting rights should be automatically restored. Roger Glegg of the conservative Center for Equal Opportunity argues for the other side in saying, "Somebody who is not willing to follow the law should not claim a right to make the law for everyone else."

Another area of contention over voting rights is whether to allow immigrants to vote before they become citizens. Arguments in favor of immigrant voting are based on the belief that if a person lives, works, and pays taxes in a country, he or she should have a right to participate in its political decisions. Those who oppose immigrant voting counter that only once an individual has become a citizen should he or she be granted the vote. This debate also exists over expatriates—people who are citizens of one country but live in another. Some contend that expatriates should not be allowed to vote in their native country because they do not live there and may not pay taxes there. Conversely, others argue that all citizens of a nation should be allowed to vote there, no matter where they actually reside.

The authors in this chapter explore who should be allowed to vote, including convicts, immigrants, and expatriates. Their arguments center on whether voting should be restricted because of criminal behavior and if voting rights should be based on residency or citizenship.

"Inmates remain part of society, although temporarily segregated, and need to be treated as citizens."

Convicts Should Be Allowed to Vote

Lukas Muntingh

Lukas Muntingh, in the following viewpoint, asserts that governments should allow all citizens, even convicts, the right to vote. Muntingh focuses on South Africa and a 2004 court decision that permitted prisoners to vote. The author concurs with the court ruling and links voting with broader civil liberties and individual rights, and contends that voting serves as an important step in rehabilitating inmates. Lukas Muntingh is an official with the South African National Institute for Crime Prevention and the Reintegration of Offenders, and a leader of the Civil Society Prison Reform Initiative.

As you read, consider the following questions:

1. According to the viewpoint, how does voting provide inmates with a "link" to civil society?
2. What were the main arguments prison officials in South Africa used to deny prisoners the right to vote?

Lukas Muntingh, "South African Constitutional Court Rules on Inmates' Right to Vote," *Corrections Today*, vol. 66, December, 2004, pp. 76–79. Copyright 2004, American Correctional Association. Reproduced by permission.

3. According to the author, limiting the rights of inmates puts society on a slippery slope to creating what problem?

Section 19(3) of the South African Constitution states that every adult citizen has the right to vote. This right, as it extends to inmates, was recently tested in February [2004] in the Constitutional Court case *Minister of Home Affairs and Others v. National Institute for Crime Prevention and the Reintegration of Offenders (NICRO) and Others*. South Africa's particular history frames the right to vote in a context that is often loaded with emotional content, while South Africans are coming to grips with the obligations (and fragility) of a constitutional democracy. Current crime levels and, particularly, violent crime do not engender sympathy for offenders among the general population.

On March 3, 2004, the South African Constitutional Court ruled on the application brought by NICRO and two inmates regarding the Electoral Laws Amendment Act that excluded inmates serving a sentence without the option of a fine from registering for and participating in the elections. Due to a convergence of circumstances, the Constitutional Court allowed the Department of Home Affairs' application direct access to the highest court of the land, without the application to the Cape High Court being decided upon, as is normally required. Each election since 1994 has seen constitutional litigation regarding inmates' right to vote.

Before looking at the results and consequences of this Constitutional Court ruling. NICRO's motivation for bringing this application and its importance within the broader context of prison reform needs to be explored.

Why Change?

NICRO and the Community Law Centre at the University of the Western Cape established the Civil Society Prison Reform Initiative (CSPRI) to address the human rights concerns of inmates and to support prison reform in South Africa through research and evidence-based lobbying and advocacy. It was through this collaborative project that litigation was initiated, using NICRO as the applicant in the Cape High Court.

The government's response to crime levels has placed the emphasis mainly on a "law and order" approach: thus, stimulating an increasingly intolerant attitude of the public toward inmates. CSPRI is deeply concerned about the general erosion of inmates' rights and this trend is not unique to South Africa; it can be observed in other parts of the world as well. The concern about the erosion of inmates' rights is based on a number of factors that informed the decision to litigate.

First, there is limited involvement from civil society in the debate on corrections and prison reform, and the quality and depth of the debate is often based on very select and dated information. In addition, there currently is weak civilian oversight in corrections and what oversight that exists is occurring within the context of widespread corruption, as evidence before the inquiry of the Jali Commission, which was established to investigate corruption in the Department of Correctional Services, continues to show. This creates a dangerously fragile environment for human rights in prisons.

At the stage when litigation was contemplated, it had been six years since the Correctional Services Act had been passed by South Africa's Parliament, but not yet promulgated in full. Limited sections, such as those relating to the Office of the Inspecting Judge of Prisons and the National Council on Correctional Services, were put into effect. It was especially the chapters of the act that described the minimum standards in relation to inmates' basic rights that remained in limbo. In the absence of a clear legislative framework that regulates prisons, there was an obligation to be extra vigilant.

Another important factor is the severe overcrowding of South African prisons that has a direct impact on the rights of inmates on a daily basis. On average, South African prisons are 68 percent over capacity, although there are individual prisons that are close to 300 percent over capacity, according to the Judicial Inspectorate for Prisons. In addition, as a result of their physical containment. Inmates have limited ability to address their concerns. While most prisons have independent prison visitors and although there are departmental complaints mechanisms in place, CSPRI is aware that much of what happens in prisons does not reach the outside world.

Finally, if inmates were to lose the right to vote, it would signal a fundamental departure from South Africans' understanding of a constitutional democracy in the post-1994 period. This could open the door for the curtailment of other rights of inmates, and possibly other sectors in the population.

Citizenship

Central to the issue of the rights of inmates to vote is the understanding of citizenship, in modern times, the imprisoned offender does not suffer "social death" leading to forfeiture of all civil rights. The history of democracy is indeed one of growing inclusion. Constitutional Court Judge Albie Sachs described this notion of citizenship in *August and Another v. Electoral Commission and Others*: "The universality of the franchise is important not only for nationhood and democracy. The vote of each and every citizen is a badge of dignity and of personhood. Quite literally, it says that everybody counts."

For inmates, the right to vote becomes a fundamental—even symbolic—link to the outside world. More important, it affirms that they enjoy protection under the constitution because they are full citizens and can participate in political decision-making. If an inmate cannot vote, what is his or her status in a democracy? Is it akin to that of a foreigner with permanent residence?

The right to vote is absolutely fundamental in a democracy and both the Canadian Supreme Court and the South African Constitutional Court have accepted this premise. Justice Arthur Chaskalson described this in the South African content in *Minister of Home Affairs and Others*: "In the light of our history, where denial of the right to vote was used to entrench white supremacy and to marginalize the great majority of the people of our country, it is for us a precious right, which must be vigilantly respected and protected."

The South African Case

The Electoral Laws Amendment Act promulgated in December 2003, provided that only awaiting trial inmates and inmates serving a prison sentence with the option of a fine would be allowed to register for and participate in elections. The result was that inmates who were serving a prison sentence without the option of a fine would not be able to register and, thus, not vote.

The Department of Home Affairs motivated this exclusion with essentially three arguments. First, the department argued that it would be logistically difficult and too costly to register all inmates. They also suggested that it would be unfair to make special arrangements for serious offenders (presumed serious because they are serving a prison sentence without the option of a fine) while the same arrangements were not being made for law-abiding citizens who could not vote at ordinary voting stations. Finally, the result would be that the message being sent out to the public is that the government favored offenders and was, therefore, soft on crime.

The Constitutional Court did not accept the cost and logistics argument for two reasons: The Electoral Commission had already visited all the prisons to register inmates awaiting trial and those not affected by the legislative amendments, and the government did not present the court with sufficient evidence to show the contrary. This left the court to deal with the issue of whether policy is sufficient reason for a limitation of rights and whether this meets the requirements set out in Section 36 of the constitution.

The Court's Decision

The Constitutional Court based its decision to declare the relevant sections of the Electoral Laws Amendment Act unconstitutional on essentially three points. First, the Electoral Laws Amendment Act resulted, in effect, in the disenfranchisement of all inmates serving a term of imprisonment without the option of a fine and this limitation of the right to vote does not conform to the requirements set out in S 36(1) of the constitution, which states:

> 36. (1) The rights in the Bill of Rights may be limited only in terms of law of general application to the extent that the limitation is reasonable and justifiable in an open and democratic society based on human dignity, equality and freedom, taking into account all relevant factors. including
>
> 1. The nature of the right;
> 2. The importance of the purpose of the limitation;
> 3. The nature and extent of the limitation;
> 4. The relation between the limitation and its purpose; and
> 5. Less restrictive means to achieve the purpose.
>
> (2) Except as provided in subsection (1) or in any other provision of the Constitution, no law may limit any right entrenched in the Bill of Rights.

The Constitutional Court has stated on several occasions that section 36 requires a proportionality analysis, which Chaskalson described, stating that what must be considered is the importance of a right against the impact of its limitation, and ask if a less restrictive measure will not achieve the same result.

In this process, different and sometimes conflicting interests and values may have to be taken into account. Context is

Voting Rights Are Key to Prisoner Rehabilitation

Giving prisoners the vote would aid their rehabilitation, which is essential if they are to avoid re-offending after being released. Denying prisoners the vote implies that they are sub-human: this damages their dignity and sense of self-worth, undermining efforts to help them control their behaviour. Voting encourages prisoners to take an interest in current affairs, which will aid their reintegration into society. Where prisoners are allowed to vote, they are usually required to vote in their home constituency, to avoid several hundred inmates in one jail causing a sudden swing in the constituency in which the jail is sited. This encourages them to take an interest in the particular community from which they came and into which they will probably be released.

George Molyneaux, "Should People Serving
Prison Sentences Be Permitted to Vote in Elections?"
International Debate Education Association, June 29, 2006.

important and sufficient material should always be placed before a court dealing with such matters to enable the court to weigh up and evaluate the competing values and interests in their proper context.

The Right to Vote

In weighing these rights and concerns as a possible justification for the limitation, the court found that the government was not convincing and was critical of its attempt to use the right to vote as a means of improving its public image: "It could hardly be suggested that the government is entitled to disenfranchise prisoners in order to enhance its image; nor could it reasonably be argued that the government is entitled to deprive convicted prisoners of valuable rights that they retain in order to correct a public misconception as to its true attitude to crime and criminals."

The court's next argument was that the state failed to provide the court with sufficient information as to why it sought to disenfranchise the group of inmates targeted and what purpose the disenfranchisement was intended to serve. Chaskalson described it as follows: "Mr. Glider [director general of the Department of Home Affairs] mentions crimes involving violence or even theft, but the legislation is not tailored to such crimes. Its target is every prisoner sentenced to imprisonment without the option of a fine. We have no information about the sort of offenses for which shorter periods of imprisonment are likely to be imposed, the sort of persons who are likely to be imprisoned for such offenses and the number of persons who might lose their vote because of comparatively minor transgressions. In short, we have wholly inadequate information on which to conduct the limitation analysis that is called for."

There is another layer to this in the sense that the entire criminal justice system is there to address crime—the police, prosecution service, courts and even prisons. But, the inmates' right to vote for those serving a sentence without the option of a fine was being presented as the final hope for addressing crime in South Africa.

The final argument was that the Electoral Laws Amendment Act provided for blanket exclusion that had long since failed scrutiny in the first *Sauvé v. Canada* case which also examined inmates' right to vote. In the absence of information explaining why these inmates are being targeted, what the potential impact of the limitation would be and how this will address current crime levels, the court was left with no option but to rule in favor of NICRO.

Implications of the Decision

The most immediate result was that all inmates were allowed to register and vote in the April 2004 elections. Given the limited time between the judgment date (March 3, 2004) and election date (April 28, 2004), there were some problems because not all inmates had access to their bar-coded identity documents. However, feedback from the Judicial Inspectorate for Prisons indicated that registration did take place in time.

Since there has been intense public debate and media attention on this matter, if this is to be used as any gauge, the conclusion has to be that the Constitutional Court did not make a very popular decision, Nonetheless, it also provided the platform for other matters regarding prison reform to be raised, especially at the time when a new Correctional Services White Paper (a policy document) has become available and the Correctional Services Act promulgated in full. The case highlighted the position of inmates in terms of their constitutional rights and the judgement raised a number of issues that are relevant to prison reform on a broader level. The most important is that should the government wish to limit any rights of inmates, it will have to pass intense scrutiny by the Constitutional Court and that the court will not be swayed by public opinion or knee jerk reaction from government.

What also resulted from the judgement is the confirmation that inmates are full citizens and are thus entitled to vote, and only those rights that need to be curtailed to implement the sentence of the court are in fact affected. Inmates remain part of society, although temporarily segregated, and need to be treated as citizens. Curtailing their rights in more ways than the absolute minimum required places society on a slippery slope of creating second class citizens. Central to the successful reintegration of inmates are human rights and approaching reintegration from a rights-based perspective, engendering a respect for the self and fellow humans. It is, therefore, not surprising to see that the Canadian Supreme

Court, in *Sauvé v. Canada*, comments on this. "Lastly, the negative effects of denying citizens the right to vote would greatly outweigh the tenuous benefits that might ensue. Denying prisoners the right to vole imposes negative costs on prisoners and on the penal system. It removes a route to social development and undermines correctional law and policy directed towards rehabilitation and integration."

International Impact

There is a growing body of local and international case law relating to the right of inmates to vote. It is clear that the South African Constitutional Court and the Canadian Supreme Court are thinking along similar lines at this stage. It should also be said that in both courts, the decision was not unanimous. In Canada, the bench was split 5–4, while two judges in South Africa dissented. Also, the European Court of Human Rights recently struck down a law that prevents convicted offenders from voting in *Hirst v. the United Kingdom*.

The relevant sections of the Electoral Laws Amendment Act were found to be unconstitutional, essentially because its blanket exclusion of a large number of inmates was not sufficiently motivated by the state. However, this decision may not be the end of the road should the government decide to make another attempt to limit this right and present a more convincing and factually based argument that meets the requirements in terms of S 36(1) of the South African Constitution.

> *"Felons are not disenfranchised based on any immutable characteristic, such as race, but on their conscious decision to commit an act for which they assume the risks of detection and punishment."*

Convicts Should Not Be Allowed to Vote

John Fund

John Fund in the following viewpoint argues that felons should not automatically be granted the right to vote in the United States. Instead, says Fund, individual states should decide under what circumstances people convicted of crimes may be permitted to vote. Specifically, the author attacks the arguments made by leading liberals in favor of voting rights for convicts and accuses them of making voting rights a racial issue. John Fund has written for the Wall Street Journal *since 1984 and is the coauthor of* Cleaning House: America's Campaign for Term Limits.

As you read, consider the following questions:

1. According to a study by Christopher Uggen and Jeff Manza, which party would felons overwhelmingly support if given the right to vote?

2. When did many states pass laws to restrict felon voting?

3. Why, according to the author, should states decide whether felons are allowed to vote?

The Constitution grants states the authority to determine "the Times, Places and Manner of holding Elections," but [U.S. senators] Hillary Clinton and John Kerry are pushing a Count Every Vote Act that would, among other things, force states to allow voters to register at the polls and declare Election Day a federal holiday. And then they want to force every state to let felons vote—even though the 14th Amendment specifically permits states to disenfranchise citizens convicted of "participation in rebellion, or other crime."

Forty-eight states deny the vote to at least some felons; only Vermont and Maine let jailbirds vote. Thirty-three states withhold the right to vote from those on parole. Eight deny felons the vote for life, unless they petition to have their rights restored, and the Clinton-Kerry proposal would force them to enfranchise felons (or "ex-felons," as Mrs. Clinton misleadingly calls them) once they've completed parole.

Support for Voting Rights

Mrs. Clinton says she is pushing her bill because she is opposed to "disenfranchisement of legitimate American voters." But it's hard not to suspect partisan motives. In a 2003 study, sociologists Christopher Uggen and Jeff Manza found that roughly 4.2 million had been disenfranchised nationwide, a third of whom had completed their prison time or parole. Taking into account the lower voter turnout of felons, they concluded that about one-third of them would vote in presidential races, and that would have overwhelmingly supported Democratic candidates. Participation by felons, Messrs. Uggen and Manza estimated, also would have allowed Democrats to win a series of key U.S. Senate elections, thus allowing the party to control the Senate continuously from 1986 until at least this January [2005].

Law Breakers Should Not Be Law Makers

The proposal to automatically restore civil rights when leaving prison would restore rights without providing a reasonable period of time to determine if felons are truly rehabilitated or still leading a life of crime. It would include felons who committed heinous offenses such as child pornography, kidnapping and luring a child, armed robbery, carjacking and home invasion, aggravated stalking, aggravated assault, and even battery on a police officer. Furthermore, the proposal would include drug traffickers who are some of society's most dangerous felons often entangled in gang violence and, worst of all, would include offenders who continually plague our society—habitual violent career criminals.

Bill McCollum, "Felons Don't Merit Automatic Rights,"
St. Petersburg Times, April 2, 2007.

Liberals normally avoid partisan arguments in expressing their support for voting by felons. Instead, they point to the disproportionate racial impact. Sometimes they overstate that impact, as Mara Liasson of National Public Radio did ... [in March 2005] when she said that "I would expect if you did a study, you would find that probably the vast majority of [felons] are African-American." In truth, a little more than a third of disenfranchised felons are black.

Felons and Racism

But that hasn't stopped advocates from raising the specter of Jim Crow [laws advocating separate but equal facilities for blacks and whites]. In 2002, the Maryland Legislature restored voting rights to twice-convicted nonviolent felons. The Old

Line State already allowed those convicted of one felony to vote after finishing parole. Sen. Joan Carter Conway of Baltimore, said any restriction was excessive: "We don't want to go back to Jim Crow. We don't want to go back to poll taxes. We don't want to go back to literacy tests."

Such arguments disturbed many moderate blacks. "By making a race issue of restoring voting rights to convicted felons, they've once again convinced many that liberal black Democrats—and probably blacks in general—are soft on, or sympathetic to, criminals," wrote Gregory Kane, a *Baltimore Sun* columnist. "That's why you would never see the NAACP [National Association for the Advancement of Colored People] of the Walter White or Roy Wilkins [NAACP leaders during the twentieth-century civil rights struggle] era advocating the restoration of voting rights to convicted felons."

The allegation that laws restricting felon voting are racially motivated is flawed. Harvard historian Alexander Keyssar, author of the classic book "The Right to Vote," points out that many states passed such laws *before* the Civil War. Later, the laws were passed in many Southern states by Reconstruction government run by Republicans who supported black voting rights. Mr. Keyssar says that "most laws that disenfranchised felons had complex and murky origins," often centering on the notion that "a voter ought to be a moral person." As one judge noted: "Felons are not disenfranchised based on any immutable characteristic, such as race, but on their conscious decision to commit an act for which they assume the risks of detection and punishment."

Let the States Decide

This is not to say that some states don't take laws against felon voting too far. Some have overly cumbersome procedures for restoring such rights. One could certainly distinguish between nonviolent felons and murderers and rapists. If I sat in a legislature in a state with a lifetime ban, I would probably support restoring the right to vote to those who had completed jail time and parole. I wonder if liberals would similarly back restoration of the right to own a gun to felons who had similarly done their time and finished parole.

In any case, it is the states that should make such decisions, based on local circumstances and debate. And the states are moving. Delaware and New Mexico recently liberalized their laws. In Connecticut, then-Gov. John Rowland, a Republican, signed a bill in 2002 that allows felons on parole to vote—a provision he can now take advantage of, since he was forced from office last year and later pleaded guilty to a federal conspiracy charge.

Careful and considered deliberation at the state level isn't enough for Sens. Clinton and Kerry. They insist on a one-size-fits-all policy that Peter Kirsanow, a member of the U.S. Commission on Civil Rights, calls "nothing less than the wholesale restoration of voting rights to convicts—and that suggests an agenda that's more partisan than altruistic."

Republicans in Congress have their own partisan motivations for opposing any enfranchisement of felons. Leaving the matter to the states probably will mean more felons regaining the right to vote than Republicans would like but fewer than Democrats desire. And that's probably about the right solution.

> *"The right to vote accompanies a person's resident status in Hong Kong, not their citizenship."*

Immigrants Should Be Allowed to Vote

Sonia Lin

As immigration increases around the world, many countries are struggling over immigrant voting rights. In the viewpoint that follows, Sonia Lin states that the right of immigrants to vote in Hong Kong is based on permanent resident status and not citizenship. However, significant restrictions are placed on who is allowed to become a permanent resident with voting rights, observes Lin. For instance, distinctions are made between the status of Chinese nationals and non-Chinese nationals. Sonia Lin is a graduate student at New York University who has worked extensively with the Immigrant Voting Project.

As you read, consider the following questions:

1. In Hong Kong, is voting tied to citizenship?

2. At what age are permanent residents eligible to vote in Hong Kong?

Sonia Lin, "Immigrant Voting Rights in Hong Kong," *Immigrant Voting Project*, August 5, 2007. Reproduced by permission. Accessed online at www.immigrantvoting.org/World/HongKong.html.

3. What percentage or registered voters participated in the 2004 elections?

Voting is a relatively recent right in Hong Kong, initiated only towards the end of the British colonial period (1842–1997) and enlarged somewhat after the handover to the People's Republic of China. For this "special administrative region" of China, the right to vote is not tied to citizenship. Chinese citizenship, after all, does *not* entitle persons to cross the border from the mainland and settle in Hong Kong, which controls its own borders and immigration policies independently from Beijing. Instead, the right to vote arises from a person's permanent residence in Hong Kong, which is a distinct concept from the person's citizenship.

Non-citizen eligibility to vote, then, is closely related to Hong Kong's immigration laws and cannot be separated from the movement for universal suffrage and direct election of the chief executive. While voting by persons holding foreign passports has gone largely unchallenged, there is some indication that increasing appeals to patriotism may make non-citizen voting an issue of debate in the future.

The colonial government started holding elections for some lower-level council positions in the 1970s, but initially restricted the vote to taxpayers with a secondary education or higher. Not until after the signing of the 1984 Sino-British Joint Declaration outlining terms of the handover did the British begin introducing substantial democratic reforms in Hong Kong. Plans for further democratic reforms were drafted into Hong Kong's Basic Law, its mini-constitution, which specified that universal suffrage and direct election of the chief executive were goals towards which Hong Kong should aspire and ultimately achieve. . . .

Who May Vote?

The right to vote accompanies a person's permanent resident status in Hong Kong, not their citizenship.

This distinction stems from the "one country, two systems" rule established with the 1997 handover of Hong Kong back to China. Although the vast majority of Hong Kongers are Chinese nationals, they have no desire to see large-scale migration from the mainland, common nationality notwithstanding. The Hong Kong government controls border and settlement policy, and only Chinese people meeting certain requirements have permanent residence in Hong Kong, with its attendant right of abode. In this political context, the right to vote is logically tied to a person's permanent residence, not citizenship.

Hong Kong permanent residence confers many of the rights that Americans might see as similar to those linked to U.S. citizenship. All permanent residents in Hong Kong hold the right to live there and, at 18 years of age, the right to vote. Both Chinese nationals and non-Chinese nationals may obtain permanent residence in Hong Kong. Non-Chinese nationals, however, must make an application for this status, unlike Chinese citizens, and they may lose their right of abode under certain conditions, such as prolonged absence.

In this respect, permanent residence for non-Chinese nationals in Hong Kong is more aptly compared to U.S. permanent residence status for foreign passport holders, albeit with voting rights and even the right to run for political office. What we see in Hong Kong, then, is a legal distinction made between groups of permanent residents who are allowed to gain or lose this status, but no distinction made between the rights enjoyed by permanent residents during the duration of their status.

Who May Not Vote?

Though non-Chinese nationals may obtain permanent residence and the right to vote in Hong Kong, in reality, many foreign residents of Hong Kong never become eligible for permanent residence.

National Fabric, cartoon by Breen. © 2006 Copley News Service.

Non-Chinese nationals ordinarily must reside in Hong Kong for seven years to be eligible for permanent residence. For many of the foreign nationals living and working in Hong Kong, however, restrictions on the definition of "ordinary residence" prevent them from accruing the necessary time to become eligible to apply for permanent residence.

Under the Immigration Ordinance, a person is an ordinary resident if s/he remains in Hong Kong legally, voluntarily and for a settled purpose, such as education, employment, or residence.

The law specifies classes of people who are not ordinary residents. These include those unlawfully present, refugees, consular officials, and people in prison or detention pursuant to any court order. These categories of restricted persons also includes contract workers from outside Hong Kong and foreign domestic helpers, the latter group of which makes up a substantial percentage of the non-Chinese population in Hong Kong.

Much of Hong Kong's population growth can be attributed to migration, and many migrants come to this Special Administrative Region of China for work purposes, often domestic work. Domestic helpers from the mainland are not allowed because of fears that this might create an avenue for circumventing the existing one-way permit system for settlement in Hong Kong.

According to government statistics, Chinese nationals make up approximately 95% of the Hong Kong population, which reached around 6.8 million in 2003. Non-Chinese passport holders number slightly more than half a million, of which the largest group were from the Philippines (2.1% of total population in 2001).

At end of April 2004, there were 220,910 foreign domestic helpers in Hong Kong, of whom 53.97% came from the Philippines, 42.17% came from Indonesia, and 2.15% from Thailand. The foreign domestic helper population increased 1.86% from the same period in 2003.

The Future of Voting Rights in Hong Kong

The extension of democratic elections in Hong Kong remains a contested issue, and the right of non-Chinese nationals to vote may come to play a more controversial role in the continuing battle between pro-democracy and pro-Beijing groups in Hong Kong.

According to some experts on the political situation in Hong Kong, the last election in 2004 was preceded by months of intimidation from Beijing, prompted largely by large-scale demonstrations in 2003 against a new security law proposed by the Beijing-friendly chief executive and later retracted. Human Rights Watch, among others, has reported on threats made against prominent anti-government media figures and the practice of some pro-Beijing employers to require their employees to use their cell phones to photograph their voting ballots as proof of voting correctly.

Turnout for the 2004 election reached its highest point ever, 55.6% of registered voters. However, because of electoral systems' design and, to a lesser degree, miscalculations in the campaign strategy of pro-democracy groups, candidates from the pro-democratic camp garnered 62% of the vote, but only got 41% of the seats in the Legislative Council.

Worries abound about whether Hong Kong's limited democracy will ever be extended to include direct elections for the chief executive and Legislative Council by geographic constituencies, as per the Basic Law. The fears of pro-democratic groups were made worse in April 2005, when Beijing announced that direct elections for the chief executive and LegCo in 2007 and 2008 will not be held, as widely hoped.

Noncitizen Voting Under Attack

The 2004 election season was marked by the launch of a debate about patriotism, where patriotism was linked to the central government and certain pro-democracy candidates and members of the press were labeled anti-patriotic for their criticism of the government.

Though non-citizen voting has not come under direct attack in the democracy debate, the issue has been debated. In November 2003, the chief of the pro-Beijing political party Democratic Alliance for the Betterment of Hong Kong (DAB), Tsang Yok-sing, spoke at a forum sponsored by the International Committee of Jurists' affiliate, Justice. In his comments, Tsang pointedly but indirectly questioned foreigners' right to vote, stressing Hong Kong's position as a part of China when discussing the Basic Law's requirement that selection of the chief executive be made in light of Hong Kong's "actual situation."

This comment touched off debate in the press and a flurry of letters to the editor of the English-language newspaper *South China Morning Post*. Tsang wrote in to the *Post* several days later to clarify the meaning behind his remarks. The right to vote was not necessarily a basic human right, he wrote. Though the right to vote is internationally recognized as a *citizens'* right, it is not considered the right of every person who lives in a particular country. He observed that Hong Kong differed from many countries because the Basic Law extends the right to vote to non-Chinese citizens, and suggested this fact be considered in deciding how Hong Kong's chief executive should be chosen. "The fact that non-Chinese nationals are entitled to vote in elections for chief executive must be an important element of the 'actual situation.'"

Should patriotism continue to be a primary theme in subsequent elections, the issue of non-citizen voting may very well arise again, potentially splitting pro-democracy groups and providing fodder and increased voter appeal for pro-government groups.

Because of its colonial past and unique political structure, Hong Kong extends voting rights to non-Chinese citizens, but voting rights of all eligible voters in Hong Kong are limited in scope. Because the future of democracy in Hong Kong remains uncertain, the future of non-citizen voting rights remains in question as well.

> "We don't want any immigrants voting
> who haven't made the conscious and
> sincere decision to renounce loyalty to
> the country they came from and pledge
> allegiance to the United States of
> America."

Immigrants Should Not Be Allowed to Vote

Phyllis Schlafly

Some local municipalities allow noncitizens to vote in city, county, and school-board elections. According to Phyllis Schlafly, not only should this be discouraged, but in most cases violates state constitutions. She believes the United States should not allow voting by noncitizens at all, as it may open the door to many problems such as allowing voting in federal elections, skewing elections toward one political party over another, or even providing cover for would-be terrorists. Schlafly is an American conservative political activist and author known for her opposition to feminism and the Equal Rights Amendment.

Phyllis Schlafly, "Felons and Noncitizens: It's All Good for Democrats," *Human Events*, August 17, 2004. Copyright 2004 Human Events, Inc. Reproduced by permission. http://www.humanevents.com/article.php?id=4813&keywords=immigrants+should+not +vote.

As you read, consider the following questions:

1. What political party would benefit from allowing noncitizens to vote?

2. What "remedy" does the U.S. Constitution provide for local governments allowing noncitizens to vote?

3. According to U.S. law, what must residents do before becoming citizens?

As the country appears so closely divided between red and blue states, Democrats are seeking oddball constituencies to enhance their numbers. They and their liberal-advocacy law firms and lobbyists have been working for months to get convicted felons certified to vote for Massachusetts Sen. John Kerry [in the 2004 presidential election] Now they want noncitizens to vote. Millions of noncitizens live in the United States, some legal and some illegal, and Democrats see this as a win-win effort to get them to the polls on Election Day. They figure the percentages are pretty good that those constituencies will vote Democrat.

Local Government Allows Noncitizens to Vote

Local decisions to allow noncitizens to vote in city, county and school board elections should not give them a pass to vote in federal elections, but once they are on the precinct registration rolls, who is going to stop them? Certainly not Democratic polling officials. In Washington, D.C., five city council members (fortunately, not a majority) recently announced their support for a bill that would allow thousands of noncitizens to vote in local and school board elections. Washington, D.C., might have as many as 40,000 resident noncitizens. That is clearly enough votes to provide the margin in a close election.

Americans need not stand by and tolerate this impertinence because, as in so many dilemmas, the Constitution of the United States provides a remedy. Article I, Section 8, gives

Some Countries That Allow Non-Citizens to Vote

Country	Restrictions or Conditions (if any)
Australia	British citizens have full voting rights.
Austria	Residents can vote in some local elections.
Barbados	British citizens have full voting rights.
Brazil	Portuguese citizens have full voting rights.
Bulgaria	Citizens of the European Union can vote in local elections.
Canada	Citizens from Commonwealth countries have full voting rights.
Cape Verde	Portuguese citizens have full voting rights.
Czech Republic	Citizens of the European Union who are permanent residents can vote in local elections.
Estonia	Ethnic Russians who are permanent citizens can vote in local elections.
Ireland	British citizens have full voting rights.
Israel	Jewish residents can vote in local elections.
Italy	Residents can vote in some local elections.
Lithuania	Citizens of the European Union can vote in local elections.
Netherlands	Residents can vote in local elections.
Norway	Three-year residents can vote in local elections.
Portugal	Three-year residents have full voting rights.
Slovenia	Three-year residents can vote in local elections.
Switzerland	Some cantons allow non-citizens to vote in local elections.
United Kingdom	Citizens from Commonwealth countries and Ireland have full voting rights.
Venezuela	Ten-year residents can vote in local and state elections.

Congress the power to pass "exclusive legislation in all cases whatsoever" over the District of Columbia, and the Republican Congress would be foolish if it doesn't act immediately to nip this mischief in the bud. The Washington, D.C., city council isn't the first to think up this thoroughly bad idea. San Franciscans will vote in November on whether to allow non-citizens, including illegal immigrants, to vote in school board elections even though this is probably a violation of the California state constitution, which requires U.S. citizenship to be eligible to vote.

Other efforts to reward noncitizens with the franchise have emerged in New York City, Hartford, Conn., Los Angeles, Colorado, New Jersey, and Texas. Scattered municipalities in Massachusetts, Maryland, Illinois and New York have already gone down this road.

No Voting Rights for Noncitizens

Giving voting rights to noncitizens is a bad idea from every point of view. It cheapens citizenship and it could give legal cover to would-be terrorists who enter the United States with hate in their hearts. There are already enough problems caused by the Motor Voter Law, under which voting registration is offered to everyone getting a driver's license. This law is in effect even in states that grant driver's licenses to illegal immigrants. Becoming a resident of a state may confer the right to get a driver's license, but it does not and should not confer citizenship.

According to U.S. law, lawful residents must speak English and swear allegiance to the United States before becoming citizens. They also must become citizens before they can vote. We don't want any immigrants voting who haven't made the conscious and sincere decision to renounce loyalty to the country they came from and pledge allegiance to the United States of America. The Constitution should also be our starting point in the matter of allowing felons to vote. The U.S. Constitution reserves the matter of voting regulations to state legislatures and, in the 14th Amendment, Section 2, specifically authorizes the disenfranchisement of felons.

Nevertheless, Democrats have persuaded activist judges to force Florida into assisting felons, as they leave prison, in getting the right to vote. The Kerry campaign has set up a nationwide legal network to recruit litigators and election lawyers to challenge election results in Florida and other close states. Democrats have been whining about people who were mistakenly listed as felons on a state database during the 2000 Florida election. But the Democrats are silent about convicted felons who actually voted illegally in the 2000 Florida election, as well as the people who received absentee ballots to vote in New York and Florida.

I suggest that those worried about whole groups of people being disenfranchised, or not having their votes counted, should consider the plight of oversees U.S. military personnel. In 2000, an untold number of military ballots were never counted. Today, about 150,000 military men and women are serving in Iraq or Afghanistan. They, above all, deserve to have their ballots counted.

Periodical Bibliography

The following articles have been selected to supplement the diverse views presented in this chapter.

Rainer Bauböck	"Expansive Citizenship—Voting Beyond Territory and Membership," *PS: Political Science and Politics*, October 2005.
Carl Bialik	"Figuring the Impact of Allowing Felons to Vote in Florida," *Wall Street Journal*, May 4, 2007.
Karen Juanita Carrillo	"Immigrant Rights Movement Affecting African Americans," *New York Amsterdam News*, April 6, 2006.
The Economist	"Out of the Cell, into the Booth," April 14, 2007.
Patrice Gaines	"Former Felons Face Uphill Battle to Regain Voting Rights," *Crisis*, July/August 2006.
Jane Junn	"Democracy for All: Restoring Immigrant Voting Rights in the United States," *Perspectives on Politics*, June 2007.
Tara Kini	"Sharing the Vote: Noncitizen Voting Rights in Local School Board Elections," *California Law Review*, January 2005.
Jamin Raskin	"Lawful Disenfranchisement," *Human Rights: Journal of the Section of Individual Rights & Responsibilities*, Spring 2005.
Ruth Rubio-Marín	"Transnational Politics and the Democratic Nation-State: The Normative Challenges of Expatriate Voting and Nationality Retention of Emigrants," *New York University Law Review*, March 2006.
Gregg Sangillo	"Ex-Felons Push for Voting Rights," *National Journal*, January 20, 2007.

CHAPTER 2

Should Voting Be Mandatory?

Chapter Preface

Voting in the United States and many other countries is considered a civic duty, but there is no legal requirement forcing citizens to vote. In some countries, however, citizens are required by law to vote. If they do not appear at the polls on election day and cast a ballot, they can be fined or face other punishments. This is known as compulsory, or mandatory, voting. Proponents of mandatory voting point out that the practice increases the number of voters, ensuring that elections are representative of the entire electorate. Countries that employ compulsory voting have much higher voter turnout rates during elections than do those nations in which voting is optional. Some contend that mandatory voting encourages people to pay attention to politics and that it is especially important in maintaining the legitimacy of governments. Author and former White House official John Dean noted the importance of voting when he wrote: "Why are citizens obliged to vote? Because government, as Thomas Jefferson set forth in the Declaration of Independence, derives its authority from the consent of the governed. That consent must constantly be renewed—through voting. If citizens don't vote, the government loses its legitimacy."

Opponents of compulsory voting argue that even in countries where people have to vote by law, voter turnout in elections is not 100 percent and turnout is, in fact, decreasing over time. They also point out that just because people have to vote does not mean that they are informed on the issues. Therefore, voting should be reserved for those who are motivated and take the time to learn about the important topics of the day. Finally, they argue, just because people show up at a polling place on election day and go into the ballot booth does not mean that they actually vote. They could simply refuse to choose a candidate or write in a non-candidate—a practice known as "spoiling the ballot" because the vote cannot be counted properly.

The following chapter examines the merits and flaws in compulsory voting. The impact of mandatory voting in other countries is analyzed, as are the theoretical dimensions of voting as a civic duty. The viewpoints attempt to determine whether mandatory voting has a positive or negative impact on democracy and citizen participation in the political process.

| "Compulsory [voting] is effective at both raising turnout and reducing turnout inequality."

Mandatory Voting Reinforces Voting Rights

Emily Keaney and Ben Rogers

In the viewpoint that follows, two British researchers argue in favor of compulsory voting in the United Kingdom. Emily Keaney and Ben Rogers contend that without compulsory voting, participation in elections will continue to decline and that such an erosion of voter turnout disproportionately hurts the poor and less-powerful groups in society. In addition, most of the objections against compulsory voting are flawed, say the authors. Emily Keaney and Ben Rogers are scholars at the Institute for Public Policy Research, a British research organization.

As you read, consider the following questions:

1. According to Keaney and Rogers, does compulsory voting lower gaps in turnout between different ethnic, economic, and social groups?

Emily Keaney and Ben Rogers, "A Citizen's Duty: Voter Inequality and the Case for Compulsory Turnout," London, U.K.: Institute for Public Policy Research (IPPR), 2006. Reproduced by permission. Accessed online at www.ippr.org/publicationsandreports/publication.asp?id=458.

2. What are the three main categories of objections to compulsory voting listed in the viewpoint?

3. According to the authors, is compulsory voting popular in countries that already enforce it?

Compulsory [voting] is effective at both raising turnout and reducing turnout inequality. Its introduction is invariably accompanied by a remarkable rise in participation. In countries where it has been enacted only in certain regions, these display more intense participation than the regions without compulsory voting. Even in countries with compulsory turnout there is still some turnout inequality, but it is invariably much less pronounced than those countries without compulsory turnout. . . .

The Impact of Compulsory Turnout

The evidence for impact on voting rates is impressive. In Europe those states with some element of compulsory turnout (approximately 18 per cent of the continent) are all situated in the top 45 per cent for turnout, and four of the top five countries have compulsory turnout regimes. In Australia the introduction of compulsory voting for Commonwealth elections in 1924 resulted in a dramatic increase in the voting levels from 57.9 per cent at the 1922 election to 91.3 per cent at the 1925 election, and turnout in Australia has averaged 94.5 per cent in the 24 elections since 1946. In Belgium turnout has averaged 92.7 per cent in nineteen elections since 1946. [In 1987 one scholar R.W.] Jackman found that compulsory turnout had the largest impact on turnout out of a number of factors including competitiveness of elections, electoral disproportionality, the number of political parties and unicameralism [having one legislative branch] versus bicameralism [two legislative branches]. Jackman argues that compulsory turnout is the only institutional mechanism that can achieve voting levels of over 90 per cent on its own. . . .

"Vote," cartoon by Harley Schwadron. CartoonStock.com

The impact of compulsory turnout tends to be greater the lower turnout is to start with. This is what makes it so important for second order elections, where turnout is generally very low. In Belgium, where voting is compulsory for provincial and local elections, average turnouts for both were just under 94 per cent between 1976 and 1994, practically the same as for national elections. In Australia while turnout is compulsory for all Commonwealth, State and Territory elections, it is only compulsory for local government elections in some states, and the degree of compulsion for these varies markedly. However, those states with the highest degree of compulsion also have significantly higher turnout rates, averaging between 85 per cent and 95 per cent.

Questions About Compulsory Voting

While this evidence is convincing and comprehensive, it does not prove causality. It could be that countries with high levels of voluntary participation are more likely to make turnout compulsory, rather than the other way around. However, within-country comparisons (before/after implementation/ repeal of compulsory voting or across sub-national units with/ without compulsory voting) still find that compulsory turnout has a large effect on aggregate voting levels with many other factors remaining constant. In Australia, for instance, in the nine elections for the House of Representatives before the implementation of compulsory voting in 1924 the average turnout was 64.2 per cent, while in the nine elections after implementation the average turnout had risen to 94.6 per cent: an increase of over 30 per cent. Similar patterns are discernable in the Netherlands where the abolition of compulsory voting in 1970 was followed by a drop in turnout of about 10 per cent.

Compulsory voting does not provide complete protection against falling turnout in mature democracies. In Belgium the number of non-voters is slowly rising despite compulsory voting, from 5.1 per cent of all citizens over the age of eighteen in 1977 to 8.8 per cent in 1995. However, this figure is still dramatically lower/better than its UK [United Kingdom] equivalent, and if compulsory turnout were rescinded in those countries where it does exist, the effect on turnout would be far more significant, following the pattern of the Netherlands. In Belgium a 1991 election study found that 30 per cent of interviewees said they would not vote again if compulsory turnout were abolished, bringing turnout to around 60 to 70 per cent.

To this point, we have been reviewing the evidence that compulsory turnout increases voting rates. This, we argued, should in turn diminish voter inequality—as a general rule the lower the turnout, the high levels of voter inequality. Such evidence as there is confirms that compulsory turnout does indeed narrow the gaps between which different groups turn out. This is powerfully demonstrated by data from the Netherlands, where the abolition of compulsory voting in 1970 resulted in a striking increase in turnout inequality. The reported turnout for five educational groups in elections following abolition varied between 66 and 87 per cent, the highest levels of turnout being displayed by those groups with the highest levels of education. This is in comparison to the last parliamentary election conducted under compulsory voting in 1967, which showed turnouts for all groups above 90 per cent. Simulations from Belgian also indicate that the fall in voting that would follow the abolition of compulsory turnout would be overwhelmingly concentrated among those with low levels of education and professional status, leading to a distortion of political representation.

Compulsory Turnout and Election Campaigns

Compulsory turnout not only increases turnout, it also cuts down the cost of political campaigning and encourages the political parties to engage with those groups least interested in politics or most dissatisfied with the political system. Where turnout is voluntary, most political parties focus on motivating their supporters to vote, rather than winning the support of undecided voters.

Both national and local campaigning tend to be directed to this end. Where turnout is compulsory, however, parties can generally rely on their supporters turning out. This can reduce the cost of electioneering and/or encourage parties to concentrate on winning over people who do not support any political party—people who often feel alienated from the political system. This in turn can increase the public's sense of political efficacy and their confidence in the political system.

The History of Compulsory Turnout

Almost all western democracies that have adopted compulsory turnout instituted it in the early 20th century, shortly after the expansion of voter suffrage and the political organisation of the labour movements. In the UK the debate has continued intermittently since the 1920s, and the first private members bill on compulsory turnout was in 1921. Objections were similar to those raised today: enforcement is costly, difficult and time-consuming and it is unethical to force citizens to vote. Nevertheless, [British prime minister] Winston Churchill, among others, supported making turnout obligatory. . . .

Objections to Compulsory Voting

Compulsory voting is a contentious issue. Even in those countries that have long-established traditions of compulsory voting there are prominent voices arguing for its withdrawal, and in some countries, such as the Netherlands, it has been withdrawn. The objections can be classified under three main categories: the right not to vote; the resultant political imbalance; and the poor quality of political decision-making produced by enforcing participation of the uninterested and ill-informed.

The most common objection to compulsory voting is that it denies people their right not to vote. The question is, even if compulsory voting does increase turnout and reduce class bias, is it legitimate, in a democratic country, to compel people to vote? And in what sense do elections conducted under such circumstances remain free and fair?

The first response to this is an important one: compulsory voting cannot, because of the secrecy of the ballot, require people to vote but only to attend the polling booth. In Belgium this distinction is made explicit in law. As already indicated, what we are really discussing is compulsory turnout. The citizen is not required to cast an actual valid ballot and, consequently, the right not to vote remains intact.

'Compulsory voting' does not, therefore, impinge on the right not to vote. However, it does impinge on the right not to take part in the political process at all. While this does represent some curtailment of personal freedom, it should be seen in context. Compulsions of one kind or another are quite usual within democratic society, from taxation, to jury duty, to the obligation to educate one's children. An element of compulsion is generally held to be acceptable so long as the resulting public good is of sufficient value. In the case of compulsory turnout, it can be argued that the benefits of increased legitimacy, representativeness, political equality and minimisation of elite power justify the element of compulsion, especially considering the relatively minor restriction of personal freedom that is entailed.

Related to this argument is the belief that compulsory turnout takes away the power to withdraw democratic legitimacy from a government by not voting. However, ... a vital part of a compulsory turnout system would be some form of formalised protest vote. This would in fact be a far more effective means of withdrawing democratic legitimacy than abstention, as it could not be misread as apathy. Compulsory turnout implemented in this way can, therefore, be seen as strengthening our democratic processes.

The Political Impact

Another concern about compulsory turnout is that it alters the political landscape. Some analysis suggests it can provide a boost to parties and policies of the left because it increases the proportions of low-income voters and these tend to vote for parties of the left. The evidence for this, however, is far from clear, particularly given decline in working class support for left parties over recent decades. In Australia, where turnout averages about 95 per cent of registered voters, [political science professor] Ian McAllister's 1986 study found that slightly higher turnout gave a perceptible boost to the Labour Party and that slightly lower turnout benefited the parties of the right, hypothesising that the abolition of compulsory turnout would strengthen this pattern and give the political right an inbuilt advantage. But simulations of the possible impact of abolishing compulsory voting in Belgium suggested that there would be little impact on overall electoral results and that the fundamental balance of power would not be altered. . . .

There is concern that compulsory turnout compels the participation of apathetic and poorly informed citizens who would otherwise abstain and are unlikely to cast a well considered vote. There is also thought to be a higher rate of invalid or 'donkey' ballots (where voters simply select the candidate at the top of the ballot). Some opponents of compulsory turnout argue that this is the cause of the large number of informal votes in Australia.

Of course it may be the case that some people would not consider their vote carefully, but no one can claim that voters in the current system base their vote on an in-depth analysis of the parties and issues at stake either; but this does not mean that they should not be included in the political process. The argument that some people cannot be relied upon to vote intelligently was also used against the extension of the franchise to women and the working classes in the 19th and 20th centuries and was rejected then, as it should be now.

It has also been suggested that far from reducing the quality of political participation, compulsory turnout may have a positive effect both on voters and political parties. A cross-national study . . . in 1997 found a small but statistically significant impact on political sophistication in countries with compulsory voting. In American and European election studies respondents interviewed prior to elections were found to vote in greater numbers than expected due to the stimulation of these interviews, suggesting that political stimulus may help to increase political interest, and the compulsion to engage with the democratic process may, therefore, increase the desire to become more informed about it.

Implementing Compulsory Turnout

Although the central objections to compulsory turnout can be countered, implementing a compulsory turnout system in the

UK would still be difficult. It would require public support to be effective. Introducing an obligation to turn out would also require reciprocal obligations from government, ensuring that voting was as easy as possible, that a public information programme was in place so people were aware of their duty to vote, and a guarantee that every vote counted. It would also require compulsory registration and an effectively enforced system of sanctions for those who did not comply.

Though compulsory turnout schemes impose sanctions on those who do not turn out, they need public backing. Without it, the sanctions would be unenforceable. Where the public backs compulsory turnout, by contrast, a relatively low level of enforcement is required. This raises the question, what does or what would the British public make of proposals to introduce compulsory turnout?

The simple answer is, we do not really know, largely because there is very little research on British public attitudes to compulsory turnout. But we do know that compulsory voting is popular with countries that have it. Australian polls taken since 1943 have shown consistent support of between 60 per cent and 70 per cent, and there seems to be little difference between major-party voters on the question.

But what research there is suggests that the British public has mixed feelings about compulsory turnout.

"The lack of interest in the vote would not somehow disappear if citizens were forced to vote."

Mandatory Voting Undermines Voting Rights

Bryan Solari

In the following viewpoint, Bryan Solari explores the problems of mandatory voting, specifically, how compulsory voting would undermine Americans' rights and damage the structures of democracy. Arguments in favor of mandatory voting, Solari says, do not take into consideration the size of the United States and the unique qualities of the American political system. The author provides evidence against mandatory voting by pointing out the negative characteristics of the practice in other countries. Bryan Solari is a musician and writer who lives in California.

As you read, consider the following questions:

1. How, according to the author, did mandatory voting in Brazil serve to alienate voters?

2. What unique features of the United States does the viewpoint contend would undermine mandatory voting?

3. Would mandatory voting be constitutional under U.S. law, according to the viewpoint?

The United States of America currently sits near the bottom of the heap concerning [voter] turnout in modern democracies. In the 2000 Presidential Election, only 51 percent of the eligible American public voted. Despite the exaggerated celebratory nature of analysts, turnout for the Presidential Election of 2004 was only higher by a small handful of percentage points. The consistent decline of voter turnout, across all electoral boundaries and in every category of election, has spurred various political scientists to ponder whether compulsory voting is a desirable remedy. Compulsory voting is the "system of laws and/or norms mandating that enfranchised citizens turn out to vote, often accompanied by (a) a system of compulsory voter registration and (b) penalties for non-compliance, usually fines or the denial of state-provided benefits." The policy's implementation has never been attempted on a national basis in the United States, and the prospective possibility carries with it numerous questions and concerns. If compulsory voting were to be instituted as law in the United States of America, indeed the structure of democracy would be transformed. However, the improvement of democracy due to the implementation of the aforementioned subject would be minimal, with the inverse negative possibilities likely outweighing any positive outcomes.

Mandatory Voting and Voter Rights

To begin to attain a proper rationale for the usage of compulsory voting in America, it is befitting to first ascertain the democratic ills that have befallen the country. As stated above, low voter turnout has become a reliable trend in American elections, with Presidential elections garnering about half of all voters, congressional elections a third, and local elections just a quarter. While this may not be alarming at first glance, several notable political scientists have given their insight as to the negative consequences of these bottom dwelling figures. Among the most active of those calling for further scholarly interest in the matter is University of California, San Diego professor, Arend Lijphart.

In his 1997 essay entitled, "Unequal Participation: Democracy's Unresolved Dilemma," Lijphart focuses on the innate discrimination that low voter turnout exemplifies on Election Day, and beyond. The major discriminatory aspects of low turnout, Lijphart contends, are along educational and economic lines. According to Lijphart, "the inequality of representation and influence are not randomly distributed but systematically biased in favor of more privileged citizens— those with higher incomes, greater wealth, and better education—and against less advantaged citizens." The consequence of his assertion is that, because the voting population consists only of the most advantaged portion of citizens, the sector of society that needs the most help is not heard through the democratic vote. The watershed of this concept is that because low-income, low-educated citizens are unable to vote for a variety of reasons related to their poverty, on Election Day their voices go unheard.

Compulsory voting has become an attractive option to political scientists like Lijphart, because the application of the policy may eliminate the very inequality of which we have just discussed. In recent election studies, the average enhancement of the vote due to compulsory voting alone has been between 7 and 16 percent. In a nation with extremely low current turnout like the United States, one would expect an even larger increase of perhaps 30 percent to occur. This is, according to Lijphart, the biggest benefit of compulsory voting, for "by enhancing voter turnout, it equalizes participation and removes much of the bias against less-privileged citizens." In other words, if by law nearly everyone in a given election zone is forced to vote, then socio-economic inequalities will diminish, because then a larger portion of the population will have had a representative input on the voting process.

By making voting mandatory and requiring the entire population to vote, compulsory voting also creates ancillary changes. For one, political scientists suggest that, "the increase in voting participation may stimulate stronger participation and interest in other political activities." Democracy is a multi-faceted system that allows for opportunity to participate on multiple, increasingly demanding levels. Thus, the hope is that by beginning with the democratic root (the vote), the level of participation in the aggregate may grow to someday embody a majority that participates in challenging political activity.

Other Benefits of Mandatory Voting

A second positive benefit from mandatory voting may be that politicians would lack the need for excessive funds. This would, in theory, prove to aid democracy because it would serve as a natural modus of campaign finance reform. Lijphart suggests that, "When almost everybody votes, no large campaign funds are needed to goad voters to the polls." A tangential outcome of this principle would also serve to eliminate attack advertising, which would potentially raise the quality of the candidates in the eyes of the electorate. There would be no need for attack advertising, hypothetically speaking, because everyone would be required to vote. Perhaps, Lijphart believes that in such a system, the attacker would be held accountable for his or her ads, and would as a result be thought of in a negative light. The reluctance to push a campaign into negative ground would probably be a welcome change for voters in the United States.

With the positive implications of compulsory voting having been displayed, we should put compulsory voting into a scheme of reality to test its theoretical value. The best representative sample for compulsory voting's transformation of a democracy can be observed within Australia.

Mandatory Voting in Other Countries

It seems that voting in Australia has benefited from the activity of compulsory voting. Because of the requirement to vote, the Australian government has made it exceedingly simple to partake in the act. In fact, according to one researcher, "voting is so easy in these well-regulated systems that failure to vote is far more burdensome than voting." The costs of not voting are essentially higher than the cost to vote on the day of the election.

The cost of not voting is financially miniscule, but morally weighted. A small fine is apparently directed at the offender, but the collection of the fine is hardly ever completed. The penalties are rather lenient, yet, voting hovers around the mid-nineties (%). Researcher Lisa Hill assumes that this is because, "Australians apparently regard it as a reasonable imposition on personal autonomy." Some researchers speculate that compulsory voting has become something of a social norm, much like other laws have become accepted as socially integrated in the United States. To not vote in Australia, perhaps, is to commit a social act of ignorance. In any case, compulsory voting has been widely accepted in Australia, and most of Lijphart's comments on the practice's effects upon democracy seem to pan out quite accurately.

The utopian conception of compulsory voting begins to fade, however, when we turn to the nation of Brazil. While not always a fully functioning democracy, the nation of Brazil does give a peek into the negative consequences that compulsory voting can create, and it is a good starting point in explaining why the practice is probably not the remedy for the democratic challenges of the United States.

Brazil, unlike Australia, had problems with compulsory voting because the system that used compulsory voting was undeniably corrupt. The corruption in government left voters feeling obviously disenfranchised and alienated, with good reason. Brazilians were in a position in 1986 and 1990 wherein the candidates and government bodies up for election were corrupt—still, to be absent at the polls was a crime. The options open to Brazilians on Election Day were unrealistically small, and indeed, in this case the mandatory vote actually helped to create a failure of democracy. Many Brazilians ended up feeling alienated from politics altogether.

On Election Day in Brazil, 40 percent of eligible voters chose to submit either tarnished, spoiled, or otherwise inoperable ballots, in what one may label a massive "protest vote." The large number of voters who chose to do so was, and is, a testament to the downfalls of compulsory voting. Stuck with a lack of choice between candidates, and little feeling of confidence in the representatives, one may assume that voters in the United States would be forced to react in such a manner, as well. To be sure, the events that occurred in Brazil exhibit the downfalls of compulsory voting that make it perhaps unacceptable and impossible to implement in the unique democracy that exists in the United States of America.

There are a number of characteristics about the United States that should be taken into account when considering the application of compulsory voting in the nation. For one, we must remember that the United States would be the most highly populated nation to attempt to incorporate the policy. In fact, this statistic alone is enough to derail the intentions of compulsory voting in America. Compulsory voting works well in Australia, but the voting population in Australia is far smaller than the voting population of the United States. In 2000, over 105 million voters went to the polls. This figure is about ten times larger than the voting population of Australia, which is no small feat. If the entire voting age population showed up at the polls, researchers would expect to see several million more.

The size of the United States, when coupled with the concept of compulsory voting, may actually damage American democracy.

Why Mandatory Voting Will Not Work in the United States

Mandatory voting is extremely unlikely to work in the states. An ABC News poll conducted this past summer [2004] found that 72 percent of those surveyed oppose the idea. The results are almost identical to a similar poll conducted by Gallup 40 years ago. Why such resistance? Perhaps because we view voting as a right, not a responsibility, and nothing is likely to alter that bedrock belief.

Also, mandatory voting would probably cause a further dumbing-down of election campaigns, if such a thing is possible. Motivated by a need to attract not only undecided voters but also *unwilling* voters, candidates would probably resort to an even baser brand of political advertising, since they would now be trying to reach people who are voting only out of a desire to obey the law and avoid a fine.

Eric Weiner, *"You Must Vote. It Is the Law,"*
Slate, *October 29, 2004. http://slate.com/ID/2108832/.*

Problems with Mandatory Voting

One common enemy of democracy is red tape. Compulsory voting would have to be coupled with auto-registration in order to even have a chance of working seamlessly in our system. With so many people voting, there would be an endless list of discouraging factors that would increase the cost of the act. The United States could probably not afford the luxury of making voting as easy a process as it is in Australia, because the sheer mass of the rush to the polls on Election Day would create roadblocks to democratic success—no matter the design of the electoral structure. When approaching the size issue from an economic standpoint, the situation looks even drearier. In Australia, the government spends an average of about five dollars per vote. Taking this into account, in a relatively small voting population the figures are contained. However, the large population of the United States would expend these costs exponentially, with even a conservative estimate figuring to cost far more.

Lijphart justifies the high cost of the election by speculating that under a compulsory voting system in America, politicians are less likely to engage in outrageous spending on mobilizing the vote. While Lijphart's point is taken, it cannot be ignored that the incentive to become elected over one's competitor would still exist in such a system. Thus, it is reasonable to assume that money would not be saved, but would rather be transferred from a general mobilization standpoint, to a partisan mobilization standpoint. According to Lijphart, "elections are therefore less costly, more honest, and more representative," but at best these are speculations that have not been proven or even tested in America.

Another problem would be the lack of choice in candidates, but the obligation by law to vote for one of the candidates nevertheless. The United States currently maintains a two party system with little room or incentive for third parties to grow or have an influence. While the expansion of the vote would probably create new third parties, most likely these parties would consist of angry, disillusioned voters. This scenario does little to promote the health of a democracy. Rather, it creates resentment against the government for providing so few choices, rather providing an inescapable pressure to show up to the polls. As we witnessed in Brazil, this situation would likely result in the failure of the democratic norm.

The Constitutionality of Mandatory Voting

Under United States law, the forcing of citizens to vote may actually be unconstitutional. According to the Supreme Court of Missouri, "voting is not such a duty as may be enforced by compulsory legislation, that it is distinctly not within the power of any legislative authority to compel the citizen to exercise it." Even if the concept were accepted as constitutional, the argument against compulsory voting would be strongly affected by the concurrent debate. Most likely, opponents would focus on the idea that compulsory voting rests on a fine line between state control of elections and democracy. The very inclusion of compulsory voting in the United States would allow the government to set up a watchdog organization assuring that people do vote, and are fined for not doing so. Thus, democracy, which depending on your definition includes the concept of free and fair elections, would be perhaps threatened by the collective power that compulsory voting would give to a government agency.

Perhaps the largest effect on American democracy caused by compulsory voting would occur across the aggregate of the voting public. Currently, the 105 million voters that show up to vote at the polls each year do so willingly, to partake in their civic duty. However, many voters today have what are known as "nonattitudes". . . .

The common belief is that while many voters suffer from this condition, the prevalence amongst nonvoters of this characteristic is far higher. Thus, compulsory voting would force politically uneducated, unwilling people to go to the polls to make a choice for President. Forcing politically inactive people to become active may seem like a logical conception, but the truth of the matter is that most of the people forced to vote will make a decision similar to a "donkey vote," and simply vote for the first choice on the ballot. Even Lijphart himself acknowledges that compulsory voting has the potential to, "force to the polls people who have little political interest and knowledge and who are unlikely to cast a well considered vote." Therefore, the above-represented situation creates a more active democracy, but it also creates a watered down system of voting wherein the quality of the vote suffers.

With the negative effects of compulsory voting on American democracy now considered, it is interesting to note another point of view on the situation. While political scientists like Lijphart believe that the implementation of such a policy would strongly improve democracy in America, and political scientists like J. Abraham believe it would drastically harm democracy, there is one branch of thought that believes it would have a far less intense effect.

Impact on Elections

Jack Citrin and his colleagues, in their article "What If Everyone Voted," considered an election for Senate in which everybody eligible to vote shows up to the polls. In a surprising finding, what they discovered was that even though an extensive number of previous nonvoters showed up to the polls in their simulations, the results were not much different. Most notably was the idea that even with many low-income, Democrat leaning voters going to the polls, the partisan effect of compulsory voting in the simulation was minimal. In some simulations, the inverse effect (a conservative bias) even occurred. According to Citrin, "while nonvoters usually are more Democratic than voters, there are exceptions to this tendency, a finding that departs from both the conventional wisdom that more electoral participation always helps the Democrats and previous scholarship maintaining that universal turnout would make no political difference." In essence, the effects of compulsory voting may not be so detrimental or beneficial outright, but with democracy going unimproved it seems senseless to change our entire system of voting to glean no reward.

On the whole, compulsory voting would indeed improve democracy if it were that democracies were judged strictly on the number of voters at the polls. Undoubtedly, millions of voters who have never voted before would join the ranks of the voter on Election Day. But the costs of statistical improvements in democratic turnout would be high, and would likely outweigh the potential benefits for the United States. The size of the United States would impair the democratic vote, and the lack of interest in the vote would not somehow disappear if citizens were forced to vote. Rather, the overall quality of the vote based on prior knowledge of key issues and candidates would be sacrificed for pure numbers.

| "Compulsory voting is likely to produce a high turnout of voters, wherever it is used."

Mandatory Voting Overcomes Problems Such as Voter Turnout

Scott Bennett

Australia has a long history of compulsory voting and averages more than 90 percent turnout in elections. In the viewpoint that follows, written by Scott Bennett and presented to the Parliament of Australia, the high turnout in Australian elections is analyzed and compared with the voting rates in other countries. Bennett asserts that while turnout in many countries with voluntary voting, including New Zealand, Canada, and the United Kingdom, has declined, turnout has remained stable in Australia and other countries with compulsory voting. Scott Bennett is a researcher with the Parliamentary Library of Australia.

As you read, consider the following questions:

1. According to the author, does mandatory voting tend to help conservative or liberal parties? Why?

Scott Bennett, "Executive Summary, Support for Compulsory Voting, the Political Impact of Compulsory Voting, the Political Impact of Voting and Turnout," *Research Brief: Compulsory Voting in Australian National Elections*, October 31, 2006, pp. 1–2, 11–16. © Parliament House of Australia 2006. Reproduced by permission.

2. As stated in the viewpoint, how much, on average, does compulsory voting increase voter turnout?

3. According to a poll cited in the viewpoint, are more British voters in favor of or opposed to compulsory voting?

Australia is one of at least 20 nations which require their citizens to vote in national elections. Despite the use of compulsory voting in Australia since 1924, there have always been opponents of the system. In the aftermath of the 2004 election, some Liberal Party members spoke of removing compulsory voting from the electoral legislation, though the Prime Minister later stated that a move to voluntary voting would not be contemplated before the next election. It is therefore likely that compulsory voting will be an issue at that election.

Critics say that compulsory voting is undemocratic, that it illustrates a tendency for over-government, that it is unfair for voters who have no preference between the parties, that it has made life easier for the parties than it should be, that it causes parties to ignore their safe electorates, and that it forces to the polling booth those whose views are not worth having and whose votes tend to increase the informal tally. To those concerned that the abolition of compulsory voting would see a drop in turnout, the critics point to what they describe as 'healthy' turnouts in other democracies which have voluntary voting systems.

Mandatory Voting and Turnout

Defenders of compulsory voting say that it increases turnout, and in doing so helps legitimise governments in Australia. They also speak of the many obligations that Australians are required to undertake, such as paying taxes or serving on juries, and ask why voting should be regarded any differently. It is claimed that in nations where voting is voluntary, a great deal of party activity (and cost) in elections is devoted to getting out the vote rather than engaging in public debate. Supporters also refer to the familiarity of compulsory voting for Australians, and ask why something that has worked well for over 80 years should be abolished.

What impact does compulsory voting have on Australian politics? What might be the consequences of its removal from Australia's electoral arrangements? The debate focuses on turnout, informal voting and the impact on parties.

Academic analysis shows that compulsory voting is likely to produce a high turnout of voters, wherever it is used. There is no doubt that the Australian arrangements produce a high figure, for Australia's is one of the most consistently high turnouts anywhere in the world—an average of 94.5 per cent in the 24 elections since 1946. The Netherlands averaged a turnout of 94.7 per cent before compulsory voting was abolished in 1971, and a turnout of 81.4 per cent in the years since. A similar drop in Australia would amount to about 1.5 million fewer voters in a national election. In the older democracies that have voluntary voting, the turnout has usually been in the order of 70 to 80 per cent, though in recent elections such countries have actually experienced a marked decline in turnout.

Criticism of Turnout

Critics of compulsory voting have claimed that an increase in informal votes in recent elections is an indication of voters reacting against compulsion by choosing to leave their ballot papers unmarked. It is impossible to be certain about why a voter chooses not to mark a ballot paper, though Australian Electoral Commission studies have shown that it is defective numbering that has been the major cause of informals, rather than the voter leaving the paper unmarked.

Some analysts believe that conservative parties tend to be the most favoured by low turnouts of voters—in Australia more Labor voters would stay away from the polls than Coali-

Countries with Mandatory Voting

Austria	Guatemala
Argentina	Honduras
Australia	Italy
Belgium	Liechtenstein
Bolivia	Luxembourg
Brazil	Mexico
Chile	Nauru
Costa Rica	Paraguay
Cyprus	Peru
Dominican Republic	Philippines
Ecuador	Singapore
Egypt	Switzerland (Some Cantons)
Fiji	Thailand
Gabon	Turkey
Greece	Uruguay

tion voters. The Australian evidence is inconclusive, however. Compulsory voting has been used for many decades, and after such a long time in use no group or party can be sure of how, or if, it would be affected by the abolition of compulsory voting.

Although some Australians no doubt resent having to attend a polling place, opinion polls have long shown that there is a solid amount of community support for compulsory voting. . . .

Increased Turnout

Academic analysis shows that wherever compulsory voting is used it increases the turnout of registered voters. One American scholar who has studied elections in the Netherlands, Austria and Australia has concluded that 'mandatory voting laws very effectively raise turnout', though he also noted that such laws 'are not a necessary condition for high levels of participation'. Another American analyst has stated that in the countries that make voting obligatory, compulsory voting 'apparently increases turnout by 6–7%'. The British scholar, Pippa Norris, currently of Harvard University, analysed the turnout of registered voters in older democracies during the 1990s, and found that those with compulsory voting experienced a turnout about 14 per cent higher than nations with voluntary voting.

Australia and Belgium

There is no doubt that the Australian arrangements produce a high figure—in fact, Australia's is one of the most consistently high turnouts anywhere in the world, averaging 94.5 per cent in the 24 elections since 1946. . . .

Australia's figures are comparable with those for Belgium, another democracy which has strictly-administered compulsory voting arrangements, and where turnout has averaged 92.7 per cent in nineteen elections since 1946. . . . Australian and Belgian figures have remained constant despite evidence that turnouts have been declining in most democracies. Various countries' returns show this quite clearly.

New Zealand

New Zealand long enjoyed a high rate of voter turnout despite its having voluntary voting. . . . Indeed, the picture did remain healthy for many years—until the last two elections surprised many political analysts. . . .

The extraordinary fall to 77 per cent in 2002 was disturbing for observers, who noted that it was the lowest turnout since electoral registration was made compulsory in 1924. It was 7.8 percentage points lower than in the previous election (1999), 11.3 percentage points lower than in the first Mixed Member Proportional election of 1996, and 20.6 percentage points lower than in the election of 1946. Judgment was withheld as observers waited for the 2005 election to see if the 2002 result was an aberration, or a sign that New Zealand was experiencing the type of fall experienced in other democracies. In fact, with only 80.9 per cent turning out in 2005, New Zealand has now recorded its two lowest figures in the last sixty years. The average figure between 1946 and 1999 was 90.3 per cent; the last two elections have averaged 79 per cent.

United Kingdom

The turnout in the 1950 British general election was 83.6 per cent; the turnout in the 2001 general election was 24.2 percentage points lower. The 2001 figure (59.4 per cent) and that for 2005 (61.3 per cent) were the two lowest returns since the 58.9 per cent in the war-time election of 1918. . . . In just over fifty years, the United Kingdom figure has thus gone from being an impressive illustration of how turnout can remain high when voluntary voting is used, to producing calls for the introduction of compulsory voting. In 2001 a private member's bill was introduced into the Parliament for this purpose, and after the 2005 election the Lord Privy Seal, Geoff Hoon, called for compulsory voting to be introduced in an effort to deal with political alienation, restore a feeling of community, and address what he called the dangerous issue of 'serial non-voters'. Claiming that international experience pointed to compulsory voting being the most effective way to increase turnout, Hoon expressed his fear that

> as the older, more regular voters die, we will be left with a significant number of people for whom voting is neither a habit, nor a duty.

In 1991 a . . . poll actually indicated that more British voters were in favour of compulsory voting than were against.

Canada

In Canada between 1945 and 1997, about three-quarters of the voters went to the polling place. The last two elections, however, have produced the lowest figures on record. . . . As in the United Kingdom and New Zealand, Canadians are concerned about this sudden slump in turnout figures. According to Fair Vote Canada, a group of concerned citizens formed in 2000 with the aim of building a nationwide campaign for voting system reform, in the 1990s Canada ranked 109th among 163 nations in voter turnout. In February 2005, a private senator's Bill to establish 'mandatory voting' was introduced in the Parliament, with the proposer stating:

> While analysts cite a variety of reasons for the voting decline including, sadly, disdain for politicians, apathy about the issues and the hectic demand of modern life, I believe that the most important factor is a fading sense of civic duty when it comes to voting participation in our democratic institutions.

"Is a government really more legitimate
if the high voter turnout is against the
will of the voters?"

Mandatory Voting Can Lead to a Range of Problems

Maria Gratschew

In the following viewpoint, Maria Gratschew analyzes the problems with mandatory voting, including the assertion that compulsory voting leads to a higher number of random votes and spoiled ballots. She argues that mandatory elections are expensive due to higher turnout and enforcement. In addition, there are a range of problems that governments face as they try to enforce compulsory voting, including how to impose penalties on those who refuse to vote. Maria Gratschew is a program director at the International Institute for Democracy and Electoral Assistance in Stockholm, Sweden.

As you read, consider the following questions:

1. According to the author, what is the leading argument against mandatory voting?

2. As stated in the viewpoint, what are "random votes"?

Maria Gratschew, "Compulsory Voting," *International Institute for Democracy and Electoral Assistance*, April, 2001. © 2001, International Idea. All rights reserved. Reproduced by permission of International Idea. Accessed online at www.idea.int/vt/compulsory_voting.cfm.

3. What are the main punishments inflicted on those who do not vote in mandatory voting systems, according to Gratschew?

Most democratic governments consider participating in national elections a right of citizenship. Some consider that participation at elections is also a citizen's civic responsibility. In some countries, where voting is considered a duty, voting at elections has been made compulsory and has been regulated in the national constitutions and electoral laws. Some countries go as far as to impose sanctions on non-voters.

Compulsory voting is not a new concept. Some of the first countries that introduced mandatory voting laws were Belgium in 1892, Argentina in 1914 and Australia in 1924. There are also examples of countries such as Venezuela and the Netherlands which at one time in their history practiced compulsory voting but have since abolished it.

Advocates of compulsory voting argue that decisions made by democratically elected governments are more legitimate when higher proportions of the population participate. They argue further that voting, voluntarily or otherwise, has an educational effect upon the citizens. Political parties can derive financial benefits from compulsory voting, since they do not have to spend resources convincing the electorate that it should in general turn out to vote. Lastly, if democracy is government by the people, presumably this includes all people, then it is every citizen's responsibility to elect their representatives.

Arguments Against Compulsory Voting

The leading argument against compulsory voting is that it is not consistent with the freedom associated with democracy. Voting is not an intrinsic obligation and the enforcement of the law would be an infringement of the citizens' freedom as-

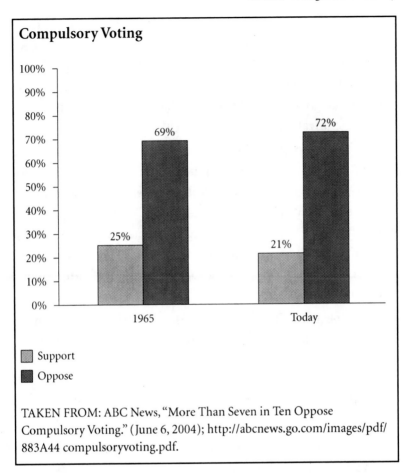

Compulsory Voting

- Support
- Oppose

TAKEN FROM: ABC News, "More Than Seven in Ten Oppose
Compulsory Voting." (June 6, 2004); http://abcnews.go.com/images/pdf/
883A44 compulsoryvoting.pdf.

sociated with democratic elections. It may discourage the political education of the electorate because people forced to participate will react against the perceived source of oppression. Is a government really more legitimate if the high voter turnout is against the will of the voters? Many countries with limited financial capacity may not be able to justify the expenditures of maintaining and enforcing compulsory voting laws. It has been proved that forcing the population to vote results in an increased number of invalid and blank votes compared to countries that have no compulsory voting laws.

Another consequence of mandatory voting is the possible high number of "random votes". Voters who are voting against their free will may check off a candidate at random, particularly the top candidate on the ballot. The voter does not care whom they vote for as long as the government is satisfied that they fulfilled their civic duty. What effect does this unmeasureable category of random votes have on the legitimacy of the democratically elected government?

A figure depicting the exact number of countries that practice compulsory voting is quite arbitrary. The simple presence or absence of mandatory voting laws in a constitution is far too simplistic. It is more constructive to analyze compulsory voting as a spectrum ranging from a symbolic, but basically impotent, law to a government which [has] systematic follow-up of each non-voting citizen and [can] implement sanctions against them.

This spectrum implies that some countries formally have compulsory voting laws but do not, and have no intention to, enforce them. There are a variety of possible reasons for this.

Lack of Enforcement

Not all laws are created to be enforced. Some laws are created to merely state the government's position regarding what the citizen's responsibility should be. Mandatory voting laws that do not include sanctions may fall into this category. Although a government may not enforce mandatory voting laws or even have formal sanctions in law for failing to vote, the law may have some effect upon the citizens. For example, in Austria voting is compulsory in only two regions, with sanctions being weakly enforced. However, these regions have a higher turnout average than the national average.

Other possible reasons for not enforcing the laws could be complexity and resources required for enforcement. Countries with limited budgets may not place the enforcement of mandatory voting laws as a high priority still they hope that the presence of the law will encourage the citizens to participate.

Can a country be considered to practice compulsory voting if the mandatory voting laws are ignored and irrelevant to the voting habits of the electorate? Is a country practicing compulsory voting if there are no penalties for not voting? What if there are penalties for failing to vote but they are never or are scarcely enforced? Or if the penalty is negligible?

Many countries offer loopholes, intentionally and otherwise, which allow non-voters to go unpunished. For example, in many countries it is required to vote only if you are a registered voter, but it is not compulsory to register. People might then have incentives not to register. In many cases, like Australia, an acceptable excuse for absence on Election Day will avoid sanctions.

The diverse forms compulsory voting has taken in different countries refocuses the perception of it away from an either present or absent practice of countries to a study of the degree and manner in which the government forces its citizens to participate.

Punishments

[There are a range of punishments for not voting, including:]

1. *Explanation.* The non-voter has to provide a legitimate reason for his/her abstention to avoid further sanctions, if any exist.

2. *Fine.* The non-voter faces a fine sanction. The amount varies between the countries, for example 3 Swiss Francs in Switzerland, between 300 and 3,000 ATS [Austrian schillings] in Austria, 200 Cyprus Pounds in Cyprus, 10–20 Argentinean Pesos in Argentina, 20 Soles in Peru etc.

3. *Possible imprisonment.* The non-voter may face imprisonment as a sanction, however, we do not know of any documented cases. This can also happen in countries such as Australia where a fine sanction is common. In cases where the non-voter does not pay the fines after

being reminded or after refusing several times, the courts may impose a prison sentence. This is usually classified as imprisonment for failure to pay the fine, not imprisonment for failure to vote.

4. *Infringements of civil rights or disenfranchisement.* It is for example possible that the non-voter, after not voting in at least four elections within 15 years will be disenfranchised in Belgium. In Peru the voter has to carry a stamped voting card for a number of months after the election as a proof of having voted. This stamp is required in order to obtain some services and goods from some public offices. In Singapore the voter is removed from the voter register until he/she reapplies to be included and submits a legitimate reason for not having voted. In Bolivia the voter is given a card when he/she has voted so that he/she can prove the participation. The voter would not be able to receive his/her salary from the bank if he/she can not show the proof of voting during three months after the election.

5. *Other.* For example in Belgium it might be difficult getting a job within the public sector if you are a non-voter, or difficulties obtaining a new passport or driver's licence in Greece. There are no formal sanctions in Mexico or Italy but possible arbitrary or social sanctions. This is called the "innocuous sanction" in Italy, where it might for example be difficult to get a daycare place for your child or similar but this is not formalised in any way at all.

> "The right to vote is only meaningful
> when you use it."

Mandatory Voting Is an Expression of Civic Duty

Mac Harb

Voter participation rates have declined in Canada. In the following viewpoint Mac Harb, a Canadian senator, explains his support for a measure to initiate compulsory voting. Harb cites civic duty as one of the main reasons for mandatory voting and equates voting with other civic responsibilities, such as paying taxes and serving on a jury. Mac Harb served in the Canadian House of Commons from 1988–2003 and has been a senator since 2003.

As you read, consider the following questions:

1. According to the the author, what crisis is causing the Canadian Parliament to consider a bill to establish mandatory voting?
2. What examples of laws intended to change behavior for the common good are given in the viewpoint?
3. What punishment for noncompliance is proposed under the Canadian measure, according to Harb?

Mac Harb, "The Case for Mandatory Voting in Canada," Speech to the Senate on February 9, 2005. Reproduced by permission of the author. Accessed online at www.parl.gc.ca/Infoparl/28/2/28n2_05e_Harb.pdf.

Our democracy depends upon the active participation of its citizens, and, while voting is only one element of political engagement, it remains the very foundation of our democracy. Reinforcing this foundation is the goal of Bill S-22, which will establish mandatory voting in Canada.

This legislation is a direct response to a rising electoral crisis. Voter turnout has been on the decline in Canada since the 1960s, reaching a record low of just 60.9 per cent in the 2004 election. Other Western democracies are also experiencing the same dramatic drop. Only 55.3 per cent of Americans voted in the 2004 presidential election, and the 2001 British general election recorded a turnout of just 57.6 per cent.

What Is Causing the Low Voting Rates?

Only one in four Canadians under the age of 25 bothered to vote in the last election. Research shows that these young people, as they age, may not re-engage in the system as their parents and grandparents did. Canadian researchers tell us that this generational shift represents a cultural change that could shake the very foundation of our democratic institutions.

Research gathered by the Association for Canadian Studies also indicates that the low turnout rate effectively disenfranchises a large number of Canadians. A study done after the last election found voter turnout ranged from 62.7 per cent to 75.4 per cent in the nine ridings [districts] with the highest average income in the country. The nine ridings with the lowest average income experienced a turnout rate from 45.1 per cent to 61.5 per cent. Whose voices are being heard? Perhaps, more importantly, whose voices are not being heard?

Renowned political scientist Arend Lijphart in the United States put it this way: "A political system with the universal right to vote but with only a tiny fraction of citizens exercising this right should be regarded as a democracy in merely a . . . hollow sense of the term."

While analysts cite a variety of reasons for the voting decline including, sadly, disdain for politicians, apathy about the issues and the hectic demand of modern life, I believe that the most important factor is a fading sense of civic duty when it comes to voting and participation in our democratic institutions.

In preparing for this legislation, I have met and corresponded with a great number of Canadians. A great many have said it is about time, and that we need this kind of signal from the government that voting is still an important element of our system. Of those opposed to the concept of mandatory voting, the most common criticism is that the bill will restrict an individual's freedom to choose whether or not to vote.

Jean-Pierre Kingsley, Canada's Chief Electoral Officer, answered this criticism best when he said, "The right to vote is only meaningful when you use it."

In Canada all citizens who are at least 18 years of age on election day have the right to vote in a general election, with the exception of the Chief Electoral Officer of Canada. We fought long and hard for this right, overcoming gender, racial, religious or administrative obstacles to ensure women, judges, persons with disabilities and prisoners in correctional facilities were given the right to vote. After years of battling for the right to vote, we have lost sight of the associated duty that goes along with this right, and that is the inherent responsibility to vote.

Voting as a Civic Duty

Voting is a positive duty owed by citizens to the rest of our society, much like paying taxes, reporting for jury duty, wearing a seat belt or attending school until the age of 16. These duties are reasonable limits we put on our freedom to ensure the success of our society.

This obligation to vote must be accepted as one of the necessary duties citizens carry out in order to maintain our system of democracy and the benefits that go with it. Other proposals for electoral reform, including lowering the voting age, proportional representation or online e-voting are all worthy of investigation, but they will not work alone.

We must change acquired attitudes and habits of Canadians when it comes to voting. Few methods work better than legislation when it comes to modifying behaviour for the common good. Seat belt laws and drunk driving legislation are excellent examples.

Despite the common perception that compulsory voting is rare, it has been used with much success. In fact, thirty democracies around the world claim to have compulsory voting, although a smaller number, sixteen democracies, use it with the level of support and enforcement we are envisioning here in Canada. These nations include Argentina, Australia, Austria, Belgium, Bolivia, Brazil, Costa Rica, Cyprus, Fiji, Greece, Luxembourg, Peru, Nauru, Singapore, Switzerland and Uruguay. Of these, the older and more developed democracies, such as Australia, Belgium, Costa Rica, Cyprus, Greece and Luxembourg, have maintained a serious commitment to institutionalize the compulsory voting law.

The Australian Model

Compulsory voting was introduced in Australia in 1924 by an appointed senator by the name of Alfred Deakin. His private member's bill was in response to the declining voter turnout of 57.9 per cent in 1922. Now, Australia has consistently boasted a turnout of over 90 per cent. Compulsory voting in Belgium dates back to 1893. Currently, voter turnout in Belgium is over 90 per cent. The most recent election in the European Union revealed the tremendous power of mandatory voting legislation and the pro-voting culture it brings along. Member states with mandatory voting during the last European Union elections had remarkable turnouts, with 90.8 per cent in Belgium, 89 per cent in Luxembourg, and 71 per cent in Cyprus, as compared with countries with no compulsory voting, voter turnout was only 42.7 per cent in France, 45.1 per cent in Spain and a mere 38.8 per cent in the United Kingdom.

These mandatory voting laws are not the hardship some might claim. Australians do not feel coerced, in fact, polls in Australia show that 70 to 80 per cent of Australians support the mandatory system.

Finally, a mandatory voting law would demonstrate to individual Canadians that the government believes voting is important and each vote has value. Nothing is more basic, but we have come to a time in our history when it must be re-emphasized.

A Proposed Law

The proposed legislation is designed to re-establish electoral participation as a civic duty in our society in much the same way legislation mandating jury duty or wearing a seat belt has ensured that our judicial system functions fairly and our personal safety is protected.

In fact, mandatory voting is not very well-named, since the only mandatory provision in the bill is the obligation to go to a polling place. Once the voter has received the ballot, he or she may mark the circle corresponding to the name of a candidate or to the words "none of the above", or simply place an unmarked ballot in the ballot box. Those who want to express their dissatisfaction with politicians or with the system by not voting will do so much more clearly by cancelling their ballot or putting an X beside "none of the candidates." Protesting by staying home can be mistakenly interpreted as being in favour of the status quo. A small fine is proposed for those electors who do not go to vote. It will simply be used to recover some of the expenses for the acquisition of supplies

Why Vote?

When I was younger I did not vote, even though I registered. I didn't care, and I didn't think my vote mattered. That changed around age 28 for me. I don't know what happened to me then, but suddenly it seemed very important to me that I start to vote. My first trip to the polls was a little intimidating, but I knew I was doing something important. I was one of the few people in my circle of friends, and even in my extended family, voting that year.

I hear many of these non-voters complaining about what is going on within the United States, and I am baffled by this. If they cared that much, they should have gone out and voted. Many argue that voting is a right not a responsibility, and there might be some truth in that. However, how can you complain when you didn't do anything to rectify the situation? You may vote, and your candidate of choice may still lose, but at least then you have earned the right to complain.

Amy Mullen,
"Should the United States Practice Compulsory Voting?"
Associated Content.com, February 21, 2007,
*www.associatedcontent.com/article/149841/should_*
the_united_states_practice_compulsory.html.

and facilities needed to hold an election. Obviously, no fine would be levied against those with a valid reason not to go to vote.

Studies show repeatedly that mandatory voting systems without a penalty simply are not as effective as those with an even minor fee for non-voting. This system does not have to be complicated. It will not cost a great deal to administer. The Australian system has shown us that small fines are sufficient to influence a change in voting patterns. In that country, if you fail to show up on voting day, you will receive a form letter in the mail requesting that you pay a fine of approximately AUS. \$20 [twenty Australian dollars] or provide a reason such as travel, illness, religious objections, et cetera. This takes care of about 95 per cent of the no-show cases. Only about 5 per cent of those who do not show up to vote in Australia pay a fine.

In the various stages of preparation for this proposed legislation, I have encountered some concern about the perceived contradiction with liberal democratic principles. I have mentioned already many other examples of mandatory tasks that we must carry out in this country. There is no denying that we have rights and that we have the associated responsibilities to go with them. We have the right to universal health care, and we have the responsibility to pay taxes to pay for that service. We have a right to a fair trial and we have a responsibility to serve on juries to protect that right. We have a right to live in a democratic society and we have the responsibility to vote to support the very foundation of that democracy.

The Right to Abstain

Canadians will still have the right to abstain. As I explained, only registered voters will be required to present themselves at the polling stations and, once there, they have the option of selecting a candidate or choosing "none of the above." They can even drop a blank ballot into the box should they choose to do so. The point is that all opinions matter and are counted, whether they are in support of a specific candidate or a rejection of the choices offered. If they are unable to vote, they need to only provide a reasonable explanation and the matter is closed.

I have also been asked about the possibility of more spoiled ballots and uninformed votes if mandatory voting were put in place. Spoiled ballots and uninformed votes have and always will be part of our democratic system. In the last federal election, about 120,000 rejected ballots were collected, almost 1 per cent of the total vote.

Once again, let us refer to the Australian example where 4 per cent of the Australian votes were rejected, not a significant number, given the much larger percentage of valid ballots cast. Some argue that it does not make sense to compel uninformed people to vote. Such exposure to the voting system may actually help them to become more informed.

As one journalist pointed out, those same "uninformed citizens" are compelled to serve on juries with potentially more serious consequences. Elections Canada has worked diligently to inform and educate voters, and these efforts will continue as an important element in a mandatory voting system.

Finally, mandatory voting would mean that voting will again become a civic duty in Canada, but not a very demanding one. Thanks to safeguards to ensure voter awareness, equality of access and the possibility of exercising one's right to vote, the bill will establish not only our right, but also our civic obligation to take part in the democratic process.

"New studies show that turnout [in the United States] has remained steady for three decades."

Mandatory Voting Is Not a Necessary Part of Civic Duty

John Samples and Patrick Basham

In the following viewpoint, John Samples and Patrick Basham dismiss concerns about low voter turnout in the United States and argue against mandatory voting. They contend that turnout is not decreasing as many studies suggest, but it has instead remained steady. In addition, the authors assert that lower turnout is a product of the unique American political system. Low turnout reflects American displeasure with contemporary politics and is therefore a political expression, not an avoidance of civic duty, they argue. John Samples is the director of the Center for Representative Government at the Cato Institute, and Patrick Basham is a senior fellow at Cato.

As you read, consider the following questions:

1. According to an estimate cited in the viewpoint, which two countries had the lowest average voter turnout rate from 1945 to 1992?

John Samples and Patrick Basham, "Election 2002 and the Problems of American Democracy," *Policy Analysis*, September 5, 2002, pp. 12–15. Copyright © 202 Cato Institute. All rights reserved. Reproduced by permission. Accessed online at www.cato.org/ pubs/pas/pa451.pdf.

2. What aspect of U.S. government does the viewpoint cite as leading to reduced voter turnout compared to European countries?

3. According to the authors, does the American system of government encourage or depress voter turnout? Why are Americans not troubled by low voter turnout?

Every election brings anguished cries about the state of American democracy. Policy activists and political scientists have argued for a generation that our nation has experienced declining voter turnout. But they have turned out to be wrong. New studies show that turnout has remained steady for three decades. Moreover, the idea that low voter turnout indicates defects in our polity can be sustained only by accepting some questionable assumptions.

Political scientists have generally measured voter turnout by dividing the number of voters on Election Day by the total population of voting age. Some have also looked at turnout as a percentage of registered voters. Measured against the voting age population turnout in presidential election years fell from its high of 62.8 percent in 1960 to an estimated 51.2 percent in 2000. As a percentage of registered voters turnout fell from 86 percent in 1960 to 65 percent in 1996.

Turnout Is Steady

But measuring voting turnout as a percentage of the voting age population leads to inaccurate figures. Recently, political scientists Samuel Popkin and Michael McDonald have shown that "voting age population" distorts turnout. The Census Bureau's estimate of the voting age population includes several categories of persons ineligible to vote: noncitizens, disenfranchised felons, persons who have moved to a new residence after registration closed, and the mentally incompetent. Popkin and McDonald have produced a new and more accurate measure of the American population eligible to vote.

The United States saw a decline in turnout between 1970 and 1974. But, since 1974, the trend in voting turnout in national elections has been basically flat during presidential years and has been slightly upward during nonpresidential election years though we have seen much variation around the overall trend. Conventional wisdom to the contrary, the United States has experienced steady turnout at the polls for about three decades.

The United States does have relatively low turnout compared with other countries. For example, one estimate calculated the average turnout in 25 countries from 1945 to 1999 and found that the United States and Switzerland landed at the bottom of the list. Although our turnout is higher than previously thought, it still clearly lags behind other developed nations.

Should the United States Have Compulsory Voting?

Should that matter? Why should the United States have the same electoral turnout as Australia or Belgium? Americans would not support compulsory voting, for example, though that would certainly raise turnout. Our separation of powers also reduces our turnout relative to European nations. We have chosen constitutionally to limit and restrain political power. Such limits make it harder to translate the wishes of the voter directly into law. Elections are thus less significant and attract fewer voters. Perhaps that is unfortunate, but the separation of powers and the general American skepticism about political power have served the nation well for two centuries. Limited government gives us both insurance against tyranny and a lower turnout compared with other advanced nations. Judging by public support for the Constitution, most Americans seem happy with that tradeoff between liberty and participation.

Voting Trends in the 2004 Elections

In the presidential election of November 2004, the 64 percent of voting-age citizens who voted was higher than the 60 percent who turned out in 2000. This was the highest turnout in a presidential election year since 1992, when 68 percent of voting-age citizens voted. The overall number of people who voted in the November 2004 election was 126 million, a record high for a presidential election year. Voter turnout increased by 15 million voters from the election in 2000. During this same 4-year period, the voting-age citizen population increased by 11 million people.

Those who decry America's low voting turnout assume citizens should be involved in politics. In the world we live in, Americans do not care much about being involved in politics. Two political scientists summarize their findings from a survey of public views about governmental processes:

Many people do not find politics intrinsically interesting. They express no desire to reengage with the political process. They do not follow most political issues because they do not care about most issues. As a result, they want someone else to take care of the political sphere for them.

Americans are not troubled by our level of voting turnout because they do not believe politics matters much. Elite commentators disagree; they think politics and democracy are crucial to a life well lived. They criticize anything other than near universal turnout as a national disgrace and set about removing barriers to voting and registration. In doing so, they show little respect for the views and values of ordinary Americans who have a right, after all, to stay away from the polls. In 2002, we can do without the biennial berating of Americans for failing to live up to the European expectations of the media and putative political experts. . . .

Contrary to conventional wisdom, across America there exists a measurable popular preference for less, rather than more, government intervention. Therefore, in the fall of 2002 an appreciation of popular sentiment will favor candidates who support defense spending, civil liberties, and smaller government outside of defense. At the same time, the political system's health is seriously weakened by a lack of competition. Unfortunately, the mismeasurement of, and pre-occupation with, voter participation serves only to distract attention from the pressing problem of an uncompetitive political system.

An election that either ushers in a new era of expanded government or further cements the advantages of incumbency will serve neither the representative nor the democratic functions of our political system.

Periodical Bibliography

The following articles have been selected to supplement the diverse views presented in this chapter.

Tom Baldwin   "We Should Force People to the Polls," *The Times* (London), July 4, 2005.

André Blais, Elisabeth Gidengil, Neil Nevitte, and Richard Nadeau   "Where Does Turnout Decline Come From?" *European Journal of Political Research*, Summer 2004.

Tilman Börgers   "Costly Voting," *The American Economic Review*, March 2004.

Derek Chong, Sinclair Davidson, and Tim Fry   "It's an Evil Thing to Oblige People to Vote," *Policy*, Summer 2005.

Bart Engelen   "Why Compulsory Voting Can Enhance Democracy," *Acta Politica*, April 2007.

Kirsten Fogg   "Law, Fine Ensure Voter Turnout," *Washington Times*, September 7, 2004.

Lisa Hill   "Low Voter Turnout in the United States," *Journal of Theoretical Politics*, Summer 2006.

Lisa Hill and Sally Young   "Protest or Error? Informal Voting and Compulsory Voting," *Australian Journal of Political Science*, September 2007.

Keith Jakee and Guang-Zhen Sun   "Is Compulsory Voting More Democratic?" *Public Choice*, October 2006.

Justine Lacroix   "A Liberal Defense of Compulsory Voting," *Politics*, October 2007.

David Mark   "Getting the Turnout, and Usually the Vote, in Australia," *Campaigns & Elections*, July 2004.

Daniel Sturgis   "Is Voting a Private Matter?" *Journal of Social Philosophy*, Spring 2005.

Should Voting Rights for Women Be Expanded?

Chapter Preface

Women were not permitted to vote through most of history. In the United States, women did not gain the right to vote until the passage of the Nineteenth Amendment to the Constitution in 1920. In many areas of the world, women continue to face discrimination in voting. Even in some developed nations in Europe, women tend to vote at much lower rates than do men. For example, in France, Italy, and Spain, women's voting rates are on average 10 to 15 percent lower than those of men. The need to increase women's voting rights is one of the world's pressing political issues. In 1897 American women's rights activist Susan B. Anthony expressed the importance of female political participation when she declared: "There never will be complete equality until women themselves help to make laws and elect lawmakers." Unfortunately, even today, women do not always enjoy the same political freedoms as their male counterparts.

In the United States, women vote now at higher rates than men. For instance, in 2000, 56.2 percent of women voted in the presidential election, while only 53.1 percent of men cast ballots. In the 2004 presidential election, those percentages rose to 60.1 percent of women and 56.3 percent of men. Nonetheless, women do continue to face hurdles in voting rights in the United States. Younger and minority women vote at much lower rates than older, white women, which may cause the issues that are important to younger, minority groups to be ignored by politicians. In addition, in some states, women do have lower voting rates than men.

Even in countries where women have the right to vote, their political freedom is often constrained in other ways. There may be cultural or political problems preventing female candidates from seeking office or the country's mainstream political parties may favor laws that restrict women's freedom.

The authors of the viewpoints in the following chapter explore women's voting rights, specifically the voting privileges of women in the Arab world, the pressure some women may feel to vote for the same candidates as their spouses or male relatives, and the bearing cultural or social traditions have on women's voting patterns. The viewpoints further analyze whether developed countries such as the United States should do more to enhance women's participation in elections and the political process.

| "Women scholars and activists are questioning key religious arguments that are being used to support discrimination. . . ." |

Women's Movements Can Help Arab Women Gain Voting and Other Rights

Leila Hessini

In the following viewpoint, Leila Hessini discusses trends in the Arab world in which, she says, women have made significant political gains and dramatically expanded their voting rights. However, explains Hessini, Islamic fundamentalism threatens many of those gains. Hessini asserts that much of the success of women's rights efforts can be credited to women's rights organizations and activists. Leila Hessini serves on the board of the Global Fund for Women and works for Ipas, a women's rights organization.

As you read, consider the following questions:

1. Women activists contend that besides elections, what are the other important components of democracy, as stated in the viewpoint?

Leila Hessini, "Strategies of Resistance: Women Contesting Islamist Movements in the Arab World," *Conscience*, vol. 27, Summer 2006, pp. 20–24. Copyright © 2006 by Catholics for Choice. Reproduced by permission.

2. According to Hessini, what are the major challenges confronting women across the globe?

3. According to the author, what is the paradox of U.S. involvement in the Arab world?

Indigenous demands for political change and democratic reform are permeating the Arab world. Pictures of women climbing through voting station windows to cast their ballots in last year's [2005] Egyptian elections were widely published as were photographs of long lines of Kuwaiti women issuing the first votes of their lives. Women have lobbied for quota systems to ensure a certain percentage of women candidates in Egypt, Jordan and Morocco. In several countries, they occupy key ministerial positions and serve as judges. Another central component of democratic processes is the proliferation of independent, nongovernmental feminist and women's organizations. (While the number of women joining Islamist groups or those who define themselves as "Islamist feminists" has also increased, this article focuses on independent women scholars and activists.) Women scholars and activists argue that democracy is not solely about elections but includes a more equitable distribution of resources and the overturning of de jure [based on law] and de facto [based on economic or social factors] gender discrimination.

Threats to Political Rights

But while women's political participation had never been greater, the Islamist winners of elections in the Arab world often seek to undermine the same democratic process that has put them in power and made women's newly achieved gains possible. Capitalizing on widespread discontent with the ruling elite and benefiting from a deep social base in mosques and religious organizations, Islamists—of which there are many types, but all can be linked by the following traits: their call for the use of Shariah or Islamic law, their fight against "corrupt regimes" and their focus on women as repositories of an ideal Muslim identity—have built an impressive electoral track record. In late 2005, the political party Hamas secured a landslide parliamentary victory in the Occupied Territories of Palestine. In the same year, the Moroccan Islamist Party of Justice and Democracy finished third in legislative elections and the Muslim Brotherhood won 20 percent of the seats in Egyptian elections—even while its leaders were jailed and election fraud was rampant. Elsewhere, Jordan's Islamic Action Front (IAF) captured a quarter of the seats in 2003 legislation elections. And the Algerian Islamic Salvation Front won the first round of legislative elections in 1990, touching off a civil war that killed more than 120,000.

While women are a quintessential focus of Islamists, the challenges confronting Arab women—including gender inequality, violence and the political use of religion—are faced by women across the globe and have nothing inherently to do with Islam. A selective and decontextualized interpretation of history—and women's roles therein—is used to support Islamists' current positions toward women. Hamas' website states that women's roles are "looking after the family, rearing the children and imbuing them with moral values and thoughts derived from Islam." The Muslim Brotherhood requires women to cover every part of their bodies except for the face and hands; otherwise they are considered "naked." Algerian Islamists attacked and killed women who held positions—such as hair-dressers or writers—that were considered "un-Islamic" and women were given two choices: "Wear the hijab (veil) or face the gun." For years, Islamists in the Gulf states blocked legislation allowing women to vote or hold elected office.

The efforts of Arab women's organizations have evolved in the context of new global and local challenges—including the rise of Islamists. Efforts to promote gender equality in the context of the increased politicization of Islam incorporate four interrelated strategies: i) breaking the monopoly on patriarchal religious interpretation; ii) challenging legal discrimination; iii) defying taboos on issues such as violence against women and iv) working to address social and economic disparities.

Divisions in Islam

Different lenses can be used to read Islamic religious texts. Muslim women scholars and activists are reclaiming the right to reread and reinterpret religious texts in light of contemporary realities and universal values. This right has traditionally been the monopoly of self-appointed religious leaders and government spokespersons who often use a patriarchal and a historic interpretation of Islam to support their positions toward women. It is usually agreed that Islam accorded women rights that were nonexistent in pre-Islam Arabia, but after the Prophet's death, conservative ulemas (Muslim scholars) codified patriarchal interpretations of religious verses into Shariah law.

Women scholars are taking the lead in distinguishing the values of gender equality and women's rights in the Quran and the hadiths (the sayings of the Prophet Mohammed) from patriarchal interpretations of Islam. Through archival research, scholars like Fatima Mernissi are unearthing women role models in Muslim history, including the Prophet's third wife, Aish'a, who participated in politics and was one of the main authorities on hadiths. These endeavors situate Quranic revelations and the hadith in their historical context and show that women served as religious scholars and imams in medieval Islam and should have the right to do so today. A woman founded the first center of Islamic studies—al-Karouine university—in Fez, Morocco, in 859 and women such as Bint al-Shati have served as renowned professors of tafir—or Quranic interpretation in Islamic universities. Moroccan lawyers Zineb Miadi and Farida Bennani published a dictionary on gender equality and women's rights in Islam. Organizations like the

Egyptian Women and Memory Forum are documenting women's voices through an oral histories project, creating new knowledge about key women figures in the past and the present and disseminating it through popular education and community outreach.

Contemporary research relies on a foundation left by earlier women activists, writers and scholars. By the mid-1920s, more than 30 women's journals existed in Lebanon and Egypt and the first women's independent and feminist organization, the Egyptian Feminist Union, was created. The Women and Memory Forum has republished the memoirs and writings of pioneer Egyptian women to demonstrate that women have been active publicly, have written from their vantage points and have been feminists. Such research and advocacy efforts show that feminist perspectives and demands were integral to Arab history.

The creation of women's studies programs in national universities in the Arab world is part of attempts to institutionalize alternative knowledge and gender-sensitive approaches. Beginning in the mid-1990s, programs were launched in Palestine (the University of Birzeit); Morocco (the University of Rabat); and Egypt (the Gender and Women's Studies Institute in Cairo).

Challenging Legal Discrimination

While most countries in the Arab world have predominantly secular laws, the personal status codes (or family codes) are derived from Shariah. These laws are based on antiquated notions of the family and women's and men's roles therein. Due to advocacy initiatives of women's organizations, governments in Algeria, Egypt and Morocco have made important reforms to discriminatory legislation, and men and women are increasingly being recognized as equals in many aspects of family law.

Women scholars and activists are questioning key religious arguments that are being used to support discrimination, including unequal rights to divorce and inheritance. Men have traditionally benefited from a unilateral right to divorce even though there is no Quranic justification for this practice. Women's groups have fought this injustice by showing that what are considered traditional laws are, in fact, modern approaches to codifying legal status between men and women.

Likewise, women have studied the historic texts and point out that women were allowed to inherit half of that of men in the seventh century—a notion that would have seemed revolutionary at the time in Europe. The rationale for unequal inheritance was that men, unlike women, had legal financial obligations. Given the likelihood that today's women earn incomes, scholars have urged reinterpretation of the appropriate Quranic verse to ensure inheritance is equally shared between men and women.

Polygamy is another focus of women's groups. While the Quran allows a man to take up to four wives, it stipulates that he can only do so if he can treat them equally. Islamic jurists are therefore divided over whether to ban polygamy, allow it with certain restrictions or allow it without restriction. Women's groups have argued that since no one is able to treat all wives equally, polygamy should be abolished. This strategy was used in Tunisia, which banned the practice in 1956; studies show that this decision has strengthened conjugal ties, reinforced women's rights and provided a context of increased security for children.

The Moroccan case bears mentioning. In 2004, it enacted sweeping changes to its personal status code due to revised interpretations of Islam and support for gender equality. The revisions include:

- increasing the age of marriage for women from 15 to 18

- establishing the right to divorce by mutual consent

- mandating that husband and wife carry responsibility for family matters

- placing polygamy and unilateral divorce by men in judicial hands

- repealing a wife's duty to obey her husband

- abolishing the requirement of a marital guardian for women to marry and

- acknowledging children's right to paternity in cases where marriage has not been officially registered

Several key elements contributed to these changes. Women scholars and activists created issue-specific coalitions to research the discriminatory aspects of the previous code and their impact on women's lives. This process engaged multiple stakeholders including policy makers, politicians, media representatives, human rights experts and women's leaders. Building pragmatic alliances was critical; in the words of Moroccan activist Rabea Naciri, in October 2005, "we were radical in our demands and pragmatic during moments of debate." Key to reform efforts was the political support of Moroccan King Mohammed VI, who also carries the religious title of Commander of the Faithful. Religious, social and legal justifications for reforms were developed; public discussions were encouraged and the media was used strategically through radio shows, talk shows and symbolic courts. Comic strips were used to raise community awareness and promote popular education.

Defying Taboos

As few reliable statistics exist on gender-based violence in the Arab world, women's groups have documented harmful practices toward women. One in three women have been victims of violence in Egypt; 51 percent and 43 percent of Moroccan

Women's Progress

Women may now vote in all Arab countries except for Saudi Arabia and the United Arab Emirates, which lack elected legislatures entirely. In 2003 women in Oman and Qatar won the right to vote and to stand for parliamentary office for the first time. And in Kuwait, after decades of debate, women gained full political rights in 2005. These reforms will encourage greater dynamism throughout Arab society. . . .

Some Arab governments resist empowering women because expanding the participation of women in politics will disperse power more widely throughout society, reducing the dominant current leaders. Quotas for female representation in political institutions, which have led to a significant presence of women into parliaments in Iraq, Morocco, Jordan and Tunisia, should be widely used throughout the Arab world as a first step toward broader equality. . . . By early 2006, women held 25.5 percent of the seats in Iraq's parliament, while in Tunisia's last elections in 2004 women claimed 23 per cent of the seats. In Morocco, the percentage of women in parliament jumped from 1% in 1995 to 11% in 2003; in the same eight-year period in Jordan it went from 2.5% to 5.5%, while in Tunisia, women's representation in the legislature rose from 6.8% to 11.5%.

United Nations, "Women's Political Participation Increasing but Still Limited, Says Arab Human Development Report, 2005," Arab Human Development Press Release, 2005, www.undp.org/arabstates/PDF2005/AHDR4_03.pdf.

women believe that violence is justified if a woman argues with her husband or refuses to have sexual relations with him. These studies demonstrate that violence is deeply rooted in societal norms—including gender roles and expectations—

and codified in legal systems that discriminate against women. Violence is often sanctioned by patriarchal interpretations of the Quran, including the belief in male authority over women. In addition to researching and analyzing the types, magnitude and consequences of domestic violence, advocates and programs are assisting women through legal aid projects providing shelters and employment for survivors of violence and training law enforcement agents, health professionals and educators to recognize the signs of violence.

Creating programs that do not treat "women" as a homogenous category but seek to respond to their different realities and needs is critical. In the occupied territories of Palestine, the Women's Center for Legal Aid and Counseling addresses both gender-based violence and the effects of increased militarization and occupation on women's lives. Groups working in Sudan have documented the systematic and deliberate abuse of women, including the use of rape, during times of war. Algerian organizations link the atrocities that were committed during the civil war to the general culture of violence that makes gender-based violence so endemic in that country. In Egypt, the organization Shumuu (meaning candles) has launched a campaign against sexual violence and discrimination of women with mental and physical disabilities.

Several innovative projects are being conducted in Morocco. Women's groups work together with a woman-headed publishing house to research and disseminate landmark studies on violence against women. Jargon-free and easy-to-read books and guides have been written by groups such as the Moroccan Association of Democratic Women and the Centre FAMA on sexual harassment in schools and universities, legal discrimination and women's testimonies of violence. Building on these efforts is Anaruz, a Moroccan national network of 20 legal aid and counseling centers for women.

Addressing Social and Economic Inequities

Islamists have been successful in the political arena because they present utopian visions of societal cohesion and provide services in marginalized and underdeveloped areas where the government is absent. Women's groups counter Islamists' conservative vision by developing programs to alleviate poverty, improve maternal and preventative health and increase access to education and labor-saving technologies. The Palestinian Development Society is developing innovative programs to address women's economic, social and psychological conditions in refugee camps. In Egypt, the Association for the Development and Enhancement of Women (ADEW) supports women's empowerment programs, including microcredit [small loans to the unemployed, the disadvantaged, or poor entrepreneurs] and women's equality in financial matters. And the Zakoura foundation has developed a network of home-based classrooms as a solution to the school drop-out rates among Moroccan girls.

Women's groups have also advocated for the protection of female workers; as a result, labor codes have been introduced that are often more progressive than those in the United States. Laws mandate the provision of maternity leave in the public sector (two months in Tunisia. three in Algeria and Egypt) and on-site day care and nursing rooms are required if a company hires more than 50 employees. Sexual harassment in the workplace is a criminal offense in Morocco.

Global Influences

While demands for democratization and gender equality in the Arab world are indigenous, they are also influenced by global politics. The region has been at the epicenter of recent geopolitical changes that have affected the world: the fall of communism, the entrenched Israeli-Palestinian conflict, 9/11 [September 11, 2001, terrorist attack on America] and its aftermath and the invasion of Iraq. In this context, the success of the Islamists is no surprise. Seeds were planted during the Cold War when the US colluded with ruling Arab elites to support Islamists to counter communist and socialist opposition. It is the logical result of post–Cold War politics where the absence of an overarching "enemy" has resulted in incoherent policies that create "otherness" where it doesn't exist and where we wage wars today against our allies of yesterday. The inversion of reality is indispensable for US strategies: war is peace, occupation is liberation and Islam is oppression. The war on terrorism is framed in language of support for "democratic reform." The paradox of the US simultaneously encouraging democracy in the Arab world while illegally invading one country and supporting the illegal occupation of another is lost on no one—and certainly not the Islamists whose social and financial base is only strengthened as a result.

The resilience of women scholars and activists and their ability to continually adapt homegrown models of feminism and activism to new global and local challenges is admirable. Women's organizations are situating their demands in a historic, cultural and religious framework that presents an alternative to the Islamists' model of what it means to be a Muslim woman. They are holding their governments accountable to universal standards and working to oppose global policies—ranging from neoliberal models of development to US interventionism—that undermine human rights. Recognition and support for independent women's groups as the bearers of some of the most progressive changes in the region could go a long way toward building true democracy—a democracy built on gender equality, redistribution of resources and a more just future for all.

> *"Iranian women faced an authoritarian regime that imposed forced veiling, gender segregation, and widespread surveillance. . . . Women resisted these policies not much by deliberate organized campaigns but largely through mundane daily practices in public domains."*

Individual Efforts Can Help Arab Women Gain Gender Equality

Asef Bayat

In the following viewpoint, Asef Bayat argues that while women have made strides in gaining rights in the Arab world, their political rights continue to be constrained. Using Iran as an example, the author describes how Arab women participated in efforts to expand democracy but often found their individual and political rights were eroded by fundamentalist Islamic regimes. Instead of gaining opportunities, Bayat says, women were increasingly repressed. Bayat suggests ways in which women can

Asef Bayat, "A Women's Non-Movement: What It Means to Be a Woman Activist in an Islamic State," *Comparative Studies of South Asia, Africa and the Middle East*, vol. 27, 2007, pp. 160–72. Copyright © 2007 Duke University Press. All rights reserved. Used by permission of the publisher.

overcome inequality other than through organized movements, which she believes are often thwarted by the patriarchal and authoritarian states. Asef Bayat is a professor of sociology and the chair of the International Institute for the Study of Islam at the University of Leiden in the Netherlands.

As you read, consider the following questions:

1. According to the author, Iranian women resisted authoritarian policies by engaging in what types of daily activities?

2. What was the literacy rate for Iranian women in 1997, as mentioned in the viewpoint?

3. When was the Bureau of Women's Affairs established, according to Bayat?

Feminists have long argued that probably all modern states possess, albeit in different degrees, patriarchal tendencies. But patriarchy figures especially prominently in those authoritarian regimes and movements that exhibit conservative religious (Islamic, Christian, Jewish, or Hindu) dispositions. Indeed, patriarchy is entrenched in religious authoritarian polity. It is known that in many authoritarian Muslim states, such as Egypt, the Sudan, Saudi Arabia, or the Islamic Republic of Iran, where conservative Islamic laws are in place, women have turned into second-class citizens in many domains of public life. Consequently, a central question for women's rights activists is how to achieve gender equality under such circumstances. A common strategy proposed consists of organizing strong women's *movements* to fight for equal rights. Movements are usually perceived in terms of collective activities of a large number of women organized under strong leaderships, with effective networks of solidarities, procedures of membership, mechanisms of framing, and communication and publicity—the types of movements that are associated with images of marches, banners, organizations, lobbying, and the like.

It is a credit to women in most Western and democratic countries for creating sustainable movements that have achieved remarkable outcomes in the past four decades. While it may be that many women under Muslim (and non-Muslim) authoritarian states do wish and indeed strive for building similar social movements, their struggles are often thwarted by the repressive measures of authoritarian/patriarchal states as well as the unsympathetic attitudes of many ordinary men. Consequently, the type of collective actions practiced mostly in the democratic settings, which have come to dominate our conceptual universe as *the* women's movements, may not deliver under nondemocratic conditions, if they are ever allowed to emerge. The conventional social movement is concerned chiefly with politics of protest, contentious politics, where collective actors exert pressure (by threat, disruption, or causing uncertainty) on adversaries to meet their demands. How does one account for women's activism that may rarely deploy organization and networking, mobilizing strategies, street marches, picketing, strikes, or disruption and yet is able to extend their choices?

In the aftermath of a revolution in which they had participated massively, Iranian women faced an authoritarian Islamic regime that imposed forced veiling, gender segregation, and widespread surveillance and revoked the pre-revolutionary laws that favored women. Women resisted these policies not much by deliberate organized campaigns but largely through mundane daily practices in public domains, such as working, participating in sports, studying, showing interest in art and music, or running for political offices. Imposing themselves as public players, women managed to make some significant shift in gender dynamics, empowering themselves in education, employment, and family law, while raising their self-esteem. They reinstated equal education with men, curtailing polygamy, restricting men's right to divorce, demonizing religiously sanctioned *mut'a* (temporary marriage), reforming marriage contracts, improving the employment status of women, bringing back women as judges, debating child custody, and to some degree changing gender attitudes in the family and in society. Women's seemingly peculiar, dispersed, and daily struggles in the public domain not only changed aspects of their lives, but they also advanced a more inclusive, egalitarian, and women-centered interpretation of Islam.

A Different Type of Activism

Not just the Islamic Republic but many other Muslim societies have also experienced similar dispersed activities, albeit with varying effect depending on the degree of misogyny [hatred of women] of the states and the mobilizational efficacy of women. Nevertheless, because of their largely mundane and everyday nature, such women's practices are hardly considered a particular type of *activism* that can follow some far-reaching consequences. How does one characterize such activities? How does one explain the logic of their operation? Drawing on the experience of women under the Islamic Republic of Iran, my purpose in this essay is to suggest that there are perhaps different ways in which Muslim women under authoritarian regimes may, consciously or without being aware, defy, resist, negotiate, or even circumvent gender discrimination—not necessarily by resorting to extraordinary and overarching "movements" identified by deliberate collective protest and informed by mobilization theory and strategy, but by being involved in ordinary daily practices of life, by working, engaging in sports, jogging, singing, or running for public offices. This involves deploying the *power of presence*, the assertion of collective will in spite of all odds, by refusing to exit, circumventing the constraints, and discovering new spaces of freedom to make oneself heard, seen, and felt. The effective power of these practices lies precisely in their ordinariness, since as irrepressible actions they encroach incrementally to capture trenches from the power base of patriarchal structure, while erecting springboards to march on. The end result can amount to a considerable modification in gender hierarchy and discrimination. This particular strategy of Iranian women to achieve equal rights offers an opportunity to perhaps rethink what it means to be a woman activist, or what may constitute a women's movement, under authoritarian regimes in contemporary Muslim societies. . . .

War and Repression

With the onset of the war with Iraq (1980–88) debate about women's status was suppressed. The authorities continued to project women as mothers and wives, who were to produce manpower for the war, for the glory of Islam and the nation. But by the late 1980s dissent simmered into women's "politics of nagging." Women complained in public daily, in taxis, buses, bakery lines, grocery shops, or government offices, about repression, the war economy, or the war itself. In so doing, they formed a court of irrepressible public opinion that could not be ignored. Then a certain iconic moment shattered the illusion of the model of Muslim women when on national radio a young woman expressed her preference for Osheen, a Japanese movie character, over Fatimah, the Prophet's daughter. Only then did authorities realize how out of touch they had become regarding women's lives in Iranian society. Some ten years into the Islamic Republic, A'zam Taleqani admitted bitterly that "poverty and polygamy are the only things that poor women have obtained from the revolution."

War and repression had surely muted women's voices but had not altered their conviction to assert themselves through the practices of everyday life, by resisting forced Islamization, pursuing education, seeking employment, yearning for arts and music, practicing sports, and socializing their children according to these pursuits. Mobilization for the war effort had already placed them in the public arena as model Muslim women, making them conscious of their power. Beyond illusions imposed by men, there were also facts. In a mere twenty years, women's unprecedented interest in education had more than doubled their literacy rate: in 1997 it stood at 74 percent. By 1998 more girls than boys were entering into universities, a fact that worried some officials, who feared that educated women might not be able to find men with higher or equal status to marry. But for young women college offered not only education but also a place to socialize, gain status, and have a better chance for jobs and more desirable partners.

Women and Employment

While for some the sheer financial necessity left no choice but to seek employment in the cash economy, most middle-class and well-to-do women chose to work outside the home in order to be present in the public realm. After an overall decline in female employment, largely in industry, of 40 percent between 1976 and 1986, the share of women at work in cities rose from 8.8 percent in 1976 to 11.3 percent in 1996. This excluded those who worked in informal occupations, family businesses, or part-time jobs. By the mid-1990s half of the positions in the government sector and over 40 percent in education were held by women. Professional women, notably writers and artists, reemerged from domestic exile; at the first Book Fair of Women Publishers in Tehran [capital of Iran], in 1997, some forty-six publishers displayed seven hundred titles by women authors. Over a dozen female filmmakers were regularly engaged in their highly competitive field, and more women than men won awards at the 1995 Iranian Film Festival. But few of their internationally acclaimed productions helped elevate the underdog image of Iranian Muslim women in the world.

Housewives Become Visible

The economic conditions of families made housewives more publicly visible than ever before. Growing economic hardship since the late 1980s forced middle-class men to take multiple

The Importance of Women in Public Life

Increasing the role and participation of women in public life is central to discussions about the development and democratization of modern states. These debates are indeed central in the Arab world because of the limited opportunities of Arab women compared to those in other parts of the world. Although women constitute more than 50 percent of the population in each of the Arab states, their participation in the public sphere is minimal. This is perhaps best illustrated by the absence of women from the parliaments. On average, the number of women in parliament does not exceed 6 percent, and the participation of women in other decision-making bodies is equally low.

International Institute for Democracy and Electoral Assistance, "Democracy in the Arab World," 2004, www.idea.int/publications/ de_arab_world/upload/arab_synth_en.pdf.

jobs and work longer hours, so that "they were never home." Consequently, all domestic and outside chores (of taking children to school, dealing with the civil service, banking, shopping, or fixing the car) that had previously been shared by husbands and wives shifted exclusively to women. A study confirmed that women in Tehran, notably housewives, spent on average two hours per day in public places, at times until ten at night, traveling by taxi, bus, and metro. This public presence gave women self-confidence, new social skills, and city knowledge and encouraged many to return to school or to volunteer for nongovernmental organizations (NGOs) or charities. One impressive example of volunteerism was the Ministry of Health's mobilization of some twenty-five thousand women in Tehran in the early 1990s to educate urban lower-class families about hygiene and birth control; mounting population growth (3.9 percent between 1980 and 1985 and 3.4 percent between 1985 and 1990) had caused the regime great political anxiety, and these women contributed to decreasing the rate to a low of 1.7 percent between 1990 and 1995.

Women did not give up on sports, even if the female body, and sports along with it, had been at the center of the regime's moral crusade. The hardship of sweating under a long dress and veil did not deter many women from jogging, cycling, and target shooting or from playing tennis and basketball or climbing Mount Everest. Nor did they avoid participating in national and international—albeit exclusively women's or Muslim—tournaments. They also defied the state policy banning women from attending male competitions; some disguised themselves in male attire, while the more assertive simply forced their way in. In 1998 hundreds of women stormed into a massive stadium full of jubilant young men celebrating a national soccer team victory. From then on women were assigned to special sections in the stadium to attend events. Their demand to play soccer in public bore fruit in 2000 when the first women's soccer team was formally recognized. Faezeh Rafsanjani, the president's daughter, played a crucial role in promoting and institutionalizing women's sports. The first College of Women's Physical Education had already been established in 1994 to train schools' sports staff.

While the new moral order and imposition of the veil had a repressive effect on secular and non-Muslim women, it brought some degree of freedom to their socially conservative counterparts: traditional men felt at ease allowing their daughters or wives to attend schools or appear at public events. Moreover, the regime's mobilization of lower classes for the war effort, street rallies, or Friday prayer sermons dramatically increased the public presence of women who would have otherwise remained in the confines of their unyielding dwellings.

Meanwhile, the women who felt stifled by the coercive moralizing of the government resisted patiently and fiercely. Officials invariably complained about *bad-hijabi*, or young women neglecting to wear their head cover properly. With a jail penalty (between ten days and two months) for improper *hijab*, showing inches of hair sparked daily street battles between defiant women and multiple moral enforcers such as Sarallah, Amre beh Ma'ruf, Nahye az Monkar, and Edareh Amaken. During a four-month period of 1990 in Tehran, 607 women were arrested, 6,589 were forced to submit written affidavits, and 46,000 received warnings. Nevertheless, by the late 1990s, the *bad-hijabi* became an established practice.

Religion and Politics

Women's daily routines and resistance to the Islamic government did not mean their departure from religiosity. Indeed, most displayed religious devotion, and many were willing to wear light head covers in the absence of force. Yet they insisted on exerting individual choice and entitlement, which challenged both the egalitarian claims of the Islamic state and the premises of orthodox Islam. Women wanted to play sports, work in desirable jobs, study, listen to or play music, marry whom they wished, and reject the grave gender inequality. "Why are we to be acknowledged only with reference to men?" wrote one woman in a magazine. "Why do we have to get permission from Edareh-e Amaken [the moral police] to get a hotel room, whereas men do not need such authorization?" These seemingly mundane desires and demands, however, were deemed to redefine the status of women under the Islamic Republic, because each step forward would encourage demands to remove more restrictions. The effect could snowball. How could this general dilemma be resolved?

The women's magazines *Zan-e Ruz, Payam-e Hajar*, and *Payam-e Zan* were the first to reflect on such dilemmas. At the state level, the Social and Cultural Council of Women and the

Bureau of Women's Affairs were established in 1988 and 1992, respectively, to address such issues and to devise concrete policies. Even Islamists, such as Rejaii, wife of a former prime minister, expressed reservations about the model of Muslim women, attacking "narrow-minded" antifemale ideas and obsession with the veil. Interestingly, many of these women worked in public office, including Parliament, and had been given a taste of discrimination by their traditionalist male colleagues. The Women's Association of the Islamic Revolution was shut down and its views attacked; the Islamic Republic Party incorporated the magazines *Zan-e Ruz* and *Rah-e Zeinab*; and once her parliamentary term ended, the prominent female Islamist A'zam Taleqani fell out of the government's graces. In the end, the rather abstract philosophical approach of Islamist women proved insufficient to accommodate women's desire for individual choice within an Islamist framework. Post-Islamist feminists, however, emerged to take up the challenge.

| "*Chilean women disprove almost all of the conventional wisdom about how women participate in politics.*"

Chilean Women's Voting Patterns Defy Assumptions

Paul Lewis

Paul Lewis in the viewpoint that follows examines the voting patterns of Chilean women. After decades of struggle, Chilean women finally earned suffrage in 1949 yet, states Lewis, they tend to defy logic and vote more conservatively than men in that country. Lewis offers examples of how women defy conventional practices, such as the tendency of women to vote for right-wing candidates. From reviewing voting data, Lewis concludes that the gender gap between female and male voting patterns is not large but it is persistent. Paul Lewis is a political science professor at Tulane University in New Orleans.

As you read, consider the following questions:

1. In what year did women become the majority of Chilean voters, according to the viewpoint?

Paul Lewis, "The 'Gender Gap' in Chile," *Journal of Latin American Studies*, vol. 36, November, 2004, pp. 719–742. Copyright © Cambridge University Press 2004. Reprinted with the permission of Cambridge University Press.

2. According to a political scientist cited in the article, do Chilean men impose their voting preferences on women?

3. According to the author, do Chilean women automatically vote for female candidates?

Chilean women won the right to vote in national elections in 1949. Law Number 12,281 of that year provided for separate registration and polling stations for the two sexes in order to allow women more freedom to vote according to their preferences. This tradition was maintained . . . in a referendum held in 1980 to ratify a new constitution, and again in 1988. . . . As democracy was being restored, . . . two new electoral laws preserved the tradition of sex-segregated voting. Law Number 18,556 provides for the separate registration of men and women. Law Number 18,700 mandates separate polling places.

The Gender Gap Before Military Rule

Women voted in four presidential elections before the military took over in 1973: in 1952, 1958, 1964 and 1970. Under the law, registration and voting were obligatory, yet women were slow to take advantage of the ballot. In 1952 only 29.7 per cent of those eligible to vote bothered to register, and of those who registered 12.4 per cent failed to vote. In 1958 the numbers were little better: 33.9 per cent registered but of those 13.9 abstained from voting. In 1964, however, the number of women who registered, as well as the number who voted, more than doubled—from around half a million in 1958 to over a million. This was still only 45.3 per cent of the eligible women voters, but among those registered abstentionism dropped to just under 10 per cent. The 1970 presidential race saw female registration rise to a peak of 1,665,988, or 47 per cent of the eligible women voters, with 86.2 per cent of those (1,436,808 voters) turning up at the polls. Their importance

Latin American and Caribbean Women Presidents			
President	Country	Tenure	How they came to power
Isabel Martínez de Perón	Argentina	1974–1976	Assumed power after the death of her husband, President Juan Perón.
Lidia Gueiler Tejada	Bolivia	1979–1980	Appointed interim president after a military coup.
Ertha Pascal-Trouillot	Haiti	1990–1991	Appointed interim president after a military coup.
Rosalía Arteaga	Ecuador	Two days in 1997	Appointed after president was declared unfit by Congress, but was forced to resign.
Janet Jagan	Guyana	1997–1999	Elected after the death of her husband, the president, to fulfill his term.
Mireya Moscoso	Panama	1999–2004	Elected president.
Michelle Bachelet	Chile	2006–	Elected president.

in the electorate had also increased apace, partly because men failed to register or vote in even greater numbers. In 1952 some 32.3 per cent of all voters were females. That rose slightly in 1958, to 35.1 per cent, and then shot up to 44.1 per cent in 1964. By 1970, women made up just under half of the electorate, at 48.8 per cent. . . .

The Gender Gap Under Military Rule

Electoral data suggest that military rule failed to shake Chilean women voters out of their conservatism. In September 1980 [military dictator] General [Augusto] Pinochet submitted his new constitution to a national plebiscite [referendum]. Since there was little opportunity for any opposition to express itself the results, in which 67.7 per cent voted 'yes' and only 31.1 per cent voted 'no', should be regarded with some caution. With that caveat in mind, it is still worth noting that 70.2 per cent of women voters cast 'yes' ballots, to only 61 per cent of men.

Much more representative of public opinion was the October 1988 referendum on whether or not to give General Pinochet another eight-year presidential term. Campaigning was more open and intense; the number of registered voters had grown from 3,539,757 in 1970 to 7,216,391 (or from 83.5 per cent of those eligible to 90.3 per cent); and the turnout rate also rose from 83.5 per cent of those registered in 1970 to 96.9 per cent. Women were now a majority of the voters (51.6

per cent) and their turnout rate was higher: 97.3 per cent to 96.5 for males. A majority of both men and women voted 'no' and so put an end to Pinochet's rule, but the male vote was more overwhelming: 58.4 per cent (no) to 39.5 (yes), whereas the female vote was much closer, at 51.1 per cent (no) to 46.3 (yes). Prior to the plebiscite Pinochet had replaced the 25 provinces as electoral units with 51 newly-drawn districts. A majority of males voted 'yes' in only 12 of those districts, none of which were in the four northernmost regions of Tara-paca, Antofagasta, Atacama and Coquimbo, where mining dominates the economy and communist labour unions have traditionally had their main stronghold. On the other hand, a majority of females voted 'yes' in 25 districts—nearly half—and in six of the twelve districts that comprise those northern desert mining regions.

Reviewing these results, Cesar Caviedes, a Chilean political scientist, concluded that they 'reiterate the established fact that Chilean female voting patterns are independent from male patterns and disprove the assumption that Chilean men impose their voting preferences on their spouses or companions'. On the contrary, 'on numerous occasions men and women have demonstrated their divergent voting behaviour, and this lack of unanimity has proved detrimental more to leftist electoral options than to centrist or rightist issues and candidates'. . . .

Voting Since 1993

Since 1993 more Chileans, of both sexes, have been failing to register. There has been a relative decline among females and an absolute decline among males. Moreover, there has been an absolute decline among both sexes in the number and percentage of those registered who actually vote in congressional elections. Since this decline is sharper among males there has been gradual increase in the percentage of voters casting a ballot who are women. Of those who vote, there has also been a sharp increase in the proportion of null and blank ballots. This reached a truly disturbing peak in the 1997 congressional elections, when over one voter in six either spoiled his or her ballot or voted for no one. This decreased somewhat in the 2001 elections, but still remained in double-digits. Throughout this entire period men were more likely than women to mis-mark their ballots or cast blank ones.

In 1989 and 1993 the percentage of registered voters who turned out to vote in the presidential and congressional elections, which were held simultaneously, was almost exactly the same. There were many fewer null and blank ballots in the presidential races, however: about half as many in 1989 and 40 per cent fewer in 1993. In each case the drop was almost exactly the same for men and women. The 1999–2000 presidential race was a different story. In the first round, only 82 per cent of the men and women presumably eligible to vote actually registered, thus continuing the decline that had set in after 1993. However, given the closeness of the race voter turnout increased: to 88.51 per cent of males and 91.27 per cent of females (compared to 87.23 per cent and 88.87 per cent, respectively, in 1997). Moreover, the null and blank votes dropped sharply: to only 2.91 per cent of male voters and 3.04 per cent of female voters, as compared to 18.70 per cent and 16.90 per cent, respectively, in 1997. With excitement at a high pitch, the second round saw an increase in voters of both sexes casting their ballots: 90.50 per cent of registered males and 91.63 per cent of females went to the polls. Null and blank votes dropped even further, to 1.96 per cent of all male votes cast and 2.07 per cent of all female votes.

Contrary to conventional wisdom, women in contemporary Chile have been less likely than men to cast null or blank ballots in most elections. This seems particularly true when high levels of such voting patterns seem to reflect feelings of protest. In the past, women were slightly less likely to register as voters, but that changed in the two most recent elections.

Once registered, women are less likely than men to abstain from voting. As voters, they consistently lean toward the [conservative] right. This does not mean that most women always vote for the right. Throughout this period the centre-left obtained majorities, or at least pluralities, from women voters. What this does mean, however, is that a larger percentage of women than men always vote for the [conservative] right, while a larger percentage of men than women always vote for the [liberal] left. There is a definite, persistent gender gap, though it is not large. Unlike pre-Pinochet Chile, it remains in single-digits.

Chilean Women and Conventional Wisdom

Chilean women disprove almost all of the conventional wisdom about how women participate in politics. Although they were slow to register and vote just after winning the suffrage, they soon became crucial participants in Chile's elections. Today they constitute a majority of all registered and active voters; and when they vote they are less likely than men to spoil their ballots. It is true, however, that women are more conservative than men, and that this holds true across all social classes. That being the case, women will not vote for another woman simply on the basis of her sex. Female candidates from the left have a more difficult time attracting women's votes than do female candidates from the right. Of course the reverse is true: men are more likely than women to vote for a female candidate from the left, but less likely to vote for one from the right.

The fact that there is a real 'gender gap' in Chile, and that it is persistent across time, region, and class, should not obscure the fact that the gap is relatively narrow. It is narrowest in the upper classes, where both men and women apparently recognise their common class interests. It is widest at the bottom of society, by around six or seven percentage points. That is not a huge gulf, although it could be critical in a close election. In general, however, men and women voters move in the same direction. In the 1989 and 1993 elections they both lent their majority support to the centre-left ticket; in the 1997, 1999 and 2001 elections they both began a shift to the centre-right. Throughout the 51 or 52 communes wherever support for a coalition rose among voters of one sex it also tended to rise among voters of the other sex as well, though not always to the same degree. Today, given Chile's recent rightward trend, it would appear that males are conforming more to female preferences than the other way around.

"*Every initiative that promotes women's access . . . must be encouraged, because gender equity is 'not a matter of numbers, but of democratic principles.'*"

Latin American Women Continue to Face Discrimination in Political Life

Kintto Lucas

In this viewpoint, Kintto Lucas reports that continuing prejudice and discrimination against women necessitates additional gender equality laws, including legislation that uses affirmative action to increase the number of female legislators and government officials. The author contends that economic equality is necessary to ensure that women gain political parity with men, especially in light of the role women play in caring for families, the elderly, and the sick. Kintto Lucas is an award-winning Uruguayan author and journalist who currently writes for Inter Press Service, an international news agency.

Kintto Lucas, "Latin America: Political Parity for Women Still a Long Way Off," *www.IPSNews.net*, August 7, 2007. Copyright © 2007 IPS-Inter Press Service. All rights reserved. Reproduced by permission. Accessed online at www.ipsnews.net/news.asp ?idnews=38820.

As you read, consider the following questions:

1. Which two countries have an equal number of men and women in their cabinets, according to Lucas?

2. In Latin American countries, what percentage of mayors are women, according to the data provided by the author?

3. According to the viewpoint, what are the three forms of discrimination that indigenous women face?

Legislation in the countries of Latin America and the Caribbean has not succeeded in ending discrimination against women in political and public life say participants at the 10th Regional Conference on Women being held in the Ecuadorean capital [in summer 2007].

The meeting was inaugurated Monday [August 6, 2007] by Ecuadorean President Rafael Correa and addressed by Chilean President Michelle Bachelet and Spanish Deputy Prime Minister Maria Teresa Fernández de la Vega. Delegations from more than 30 countries were present.

The present governments of both Chile and Spain began their administrations with gender parity in their cabinets: equal numbers of women and men in charge of ministries.

Bachelet said that although her election as president was a "defeat for exclusion and a victory for inclusion," and in Chile her government is making efforts to achieve "parity in political and public representation" for men and women, there is still much to be done to overcome the remaining "prejudices."

Every initiative that promotes women's access to "public and political representation" must be encouraged, because gender equity "is not a question of numbers, but of democratic principles," she added.

Quota Laws

Quota laws to establish mandatory proportions of women in political bodies and on lists of electoral candidates, as well as

Women's Suffrage in Latin America and the Caribbean			
Country	**Date of Suffrage**	**Country**	**Date of Suffrage**
Guyana	1928	Surinam	1948
Ecuador	1929	Costa Rica	1949
Chile	1931 (Initially limited)	Barbados	1950
Brazil	1934	Haiti	1950
Cuba	1934	Antigua	1951
El Salvador	1939	Grenada	1951
Panama	1941 (Initially limited)	Belize	1954
Dominican Republic	1942	Colombia	1954
Jamaica	1944	Honduras	1955
Guatemala	1946	Nicaragua	1955
Argentina	1947	Peru	1955
Mexico	1947 (Initially limited)	Bahamas	1961

other affirmative action initiatives, all help towards finally overcoming exclusion, she said.

Therefore, Bachelet will send a draft law to the Chilean Congress in September [2007] to establish minimum quotas for women candidates for elected posts, she announced.

In her view, women's participation in the workforce, the changes in their domestic relationships, and their opportunities to hold "positions of authority" in many countries, constitute the main revolution of the 20th century.

"More women, more democracy, more justice. Equality is not just a dream," Bachelet concluded, to applause from the hundreds of participants.

Fernández de la Vega, meanwhile, said she subscribed to a "democratic and feminist" world view, and said that millions of women are heavily burdened by injustice because they are regarded as second class citizens.

Economic Equality

In addition to political parity, equality in employment is needed, to end "the old sexual division of labour," said Fernández de la Vega.

Implementing laws and state policies that do away with unpaid domestic labour, which is carried out by millions of women, is a fundamental requirement, she said.

"Women have taken on responsibility for caring for others, and people have assumed that this is natural, whereas it is not, so it is essential to develop policies to address society's public responsibility" for this work, she said.

"We need to recognise the value of women's contribution to the economy and to social cohesion through the unpaid domestic work they do, and at the same time we need to put forward proposals for it to be solved and shared differently. These tasks are a priority," she said.

Similarly, "it is essential to continue to work for a full, inclusive democracy, characterised by gender equity, that incorporates women at all levels of decision-making, in order to end an injustice that has lasted for centuries, and to restore women's full citizenship rights," Fernández de la Vega said.

A study by the United Nations International Research and Training Institute for the Advancement of Women (UN-INSTRAW) found that, although political participation by women has increased over the last decade in Latin America, the situation is still a long way from gender parity.

In the executive branch in the region, the proportion of women rose from nine to 14 percent in 10 years. In the Senate, it grew from five to 13 percent, and in the lower chambers from eight to 15 percent.

But at the municipal level, where representation and governance is closest to the populace and to everyday life, the proportion of women is much lower and has not grown significantly in the last 10 years, according to UN-INSTRAW.

Data collected by UN-INSTRAW in 16 Latin American countries indicate that only 5.3 percent of mayors are women, in 842 out of 15,828 local governments.

"In the local sphere, there is a worrying paradox: the municipality is the space where women participate most in economic, social and cultural life. But also it is where few occupy political positions," said Carmen Moreno, head of UN-INSTRAW.

In countries where there are quota laws for the inclusion of specified proportions of women on candidate lists for municipal elections, there has been a marked increase in the number of town councillors, Moreno said.

However, the mechanism does not apply to mayoral elections, where candidates stand as individuals. The office of mayor continues to be almost exclusively dominated by men.

Indigenous Peoples

Ecuadorean indigenous leader Blanca Chancoso told IPS [Inter Press Service] that discrimination in the political and public sphere is much greater for women who are poor and of indigenous or African descent.

Inequality in politics also has "a social class and ethnic component which needs to be taken into account," Chancoso said.

The long-time leader of the Ecuadorean indigenous people's movement said that poor indigenous and black people have far less chances of being elected to a public position.

This is corroborated by another UN-INSTRAW study, which says that indigenous women experience access to resources and positions of power in a different way from non-indigenous men and women.

Women account for nearly 60 percent of the 50 million indigenous people in Latin America and the Caribbean, and they face triple discrimination: as women, as indigenous people and as poor people, the study says.

In Bolivia, Colombia, Ecuador, Guatemala and Peru, where at least half of women are indigenous, the obstacles are related to conservative traditions, lack of basic identity documents, a low literacy rate, lack of access to financial resources, lack of opportunities for capacity-building, and centralised exercise of power, among other aspects, the study says.

The conference in Quito [Ecuador] . . . is the most important intergovernmental forum for analysing public policies on gender and is convened every three years by the Economic Commission for Latin America and the Caribbean (ECLAC).

This year the conference is focussing on the contribution of women's unpaid work to the economy and social protection, and on political participation and gender parity.

In his welcoming speech, President Correa said he hoped the next Ecuadorean government would have a woman president.

"We cannot talk about development while gender discrimination continues," he said. "'On the street, arm in arm, we are so much more than two,' (Uruguayan poet) Mario Benedetti said. You are the women's faces of this region, and you are welcome," he said.

"While their European and American sisters were being jailed and abused for demanding the right to vote, Ottoman women organized into powerful political groups."

Women Have Extensive Voting Rights in Some Countries

Turkuaz

In this viewpoint, the editors of the journal Turkuaz *discuss the political freedom and voting rights of women in Turkey. Unlike some common misperceptions, say the authors, Turkey is a modern secular state where women have significant political rights under the law. In fact, Turkish women earned the right to vote before women in the European countries of Italy, France, Belgium, Greece, and Portugal. Even today, in some respects, Turkish women are better integrated than their European or American counterparts, argue the editors. The viewpoint traces the rise of women's rights and its impact on modern Turkish society.* Turkuaz *is an English-language journal that is published in print and online.*

"European Ignorance 'Unveiled'," *Turkuaz Magazine*, Spring 2005. © Turkuaz Productions, LLC. 2002–2007. Reproduced by permission. Accessed online at http://turkuaz.us/content.php?magId=8.

As you read, consider the following questions:

1. In what year did Ottoman women gain the right to higher education in law, according to the viewpoint?
2. Who does the author reveal led the effort in 1923 to promote women's rights in Turkey?
3. What reasons does the author give for European Union opposition to Turkish membership in the organization?

'She sat demurely. Her long hair, glittering bronze eyes, thin waist and playful tail concealed by a dark burka, the traditional Afghani Muslim dress' made headlines on the eve of the U.S.-led invasion of that country. 'Turkey in the EU [European Union]?' read the bold sign that was hung around her shoulders. On December 17, 2004, the bronze statue of The Little Mermaid, Denmark's national symbol, had turned overnight into a charged and highly misleading symbol of protest against Turkey's possible entry into the European Union.

Aside from the irony of the sexist Danish tale of The Little Mermaid, in which a young mermaid sacrifices her life for a foolish prince, the image deserves our attention because it shows just how little the Danish, and by extension Western Europeans, really know about Turkey. Turkish women who choose to manifest their religious belief by covering themselves rarely wear the black chador, and never wear the much more restrictive burka. Instead, they typically prefer a simple headscarf, just as some religious Catholics do. And the rest of the women in modern-day Turkey dress much more liberally than most American women do. Perhaps if the Danes knew more women in modern-day Turkey, 49 percent of Danish citizens would not oppose Turkey's entry into the EU, as reported in Denmark's leading daily *Jyllands-Posten*. It seems that Europeans, who regularly criticize American ignorance of other countries, are quite capable of engaging in politically strategic ignorance themselves.

Equal Rights in Turkey

Ironically, Atatürk's [Mustafa Atatürk, the founder and first president of the Republic of Turkey] endowment of equal rights to Turkish women is completely taken for granted in Turkey. Turkish feminists even complain that, because Turkish women never had to ask for the rights they currently enjoy, there never was and can never be a powerful Turkish women's movement. And now, as the right-leaning governing party . . . makes amendments to the Turkish Civil Code, Turkish women are once again being granted freedom and equality by a benevolent male force.

Westerners haven't always had so many misgivings about the status of women in Turkish society. According to feminist scholar Anouvar Majid, before the 20th century, Western women were fascinated by the rights and privileges enjoyed by Ottoman women of all classes. Lady Mary Wortley Montagu, wife of the British ambassador to the Ottoman Empire, wrote in the 18th century that she 'never saw a country where women may enjoy so much liberty, and free from all reproach, as in Turkey.' She noted in 1717 that property law in Islamic Ottoman society was fairer to women than that of Western societies. 'The Turkish woman does not fear her husband, because she owns her own property.' In fact, according to Majid, English women cited their envy of the equality granted to Turkish women in almost every sphere of social life as late as the 19th century. For example, author Mary Lucy Garnet, in her 1893 book called *Women of Turkey and Their Folklore*, praised Ottoman Muslim women and denounced European state-enforced misogyny [hatred of women].

Ottoman women by no means enjoyed 'equal rights' as they are currently defined by liberal democracies, but they were hardly, as some Turkish feminists argue, passive bystanders to their political destiny. While their European and American sisters were being jailed and abused for demanding the right to vote, Ottoman women organized into powerful political groups.

Throughout the 19th century, Ottoman women owned and published women's magazines, in which they celebrated the successes of Muslim women, argued for women's right to higher education, and publicized the works of female novelists and poets. Thanks to their efforts, the Ottoman constitution was continuously amended during the early 20th century in favor of more equality for women, banning unequal punishment for adultery and necessitating women's consent for polygamous marriages—a reform many contemporary Islamic countries have yet to make. During this time, with the help of female activists and intellectuals, such as the famous poet Tevfik Fikret, Ottoman women gained the right to higher education, enjoying co-ed professional education in law as early as 1912. The early 20th century also gave Turkey its first modern feminist: Halide Edip Adivar, a renowned novelist, professor, and politician who led the Ottoman women's movement. She founded the Society for the Elevation of Women in 1908, dedicating herself to the improvement of education opportunities for Turkish women, and to improving relations between Turkish women and European women. But despite these significant strides toward full equality, Islamic Shariah law [based on the teachings of the Koran, the Muslim holy book] prevented full legal equality from developing.

The New Republic

Once the Independence War ended, Atatürk decreed that the new Turkish Republic would finally extend full citizenship to its daughters, famously proclaiming in 1923 that, 'The reason for the failure of our social body is our past neglect of our women. To live is to function. Therefore, if, in a social body, an organ functions while the other one doesn't, that society is paralyzed.'

Pioneers in Women's Rights

Seen from an international perspective, the history of women's suffrage contains an interesting paradox: the more vehement the battle, the more meagre the results. Countries with the most militant suffragettism had to wait for years, even decades, before they could enjoy the fruits of their struggle, while many small, peripheral countries gave women full parliamentary representation at an early date without much ado. New Zealand was the pioneer, accepting women's right to vote in 1893, followed by Australia in 1902, while Finland was the European forerunner in 1906. Finland's thoroughgoing parliamentary reforms gave all adult men and women not only universal and equal suffrage, but also the full right to stand for elective office. This was unprecedented in the whole world.

Irma Sulkunen,
Virtual Finland, *June 2000.*

Atatürk's belief in equality for women was not only un-usual for his time, it was also quite sincere. Janet Browning, author of *Atatürk's Legacy to the Women of Turkey,* quotes a personal note he made on his copy of the play Stone Doll, fol-lowing a character's suggestion that women are like orna-ments. 'We cannot think of women this way!,' Atatürk wrote. 'The presence of women is fundamental to the nation on a thousand and one points. It is not right to go on renewing the idea that woman is an ornament.'

The improvement of the legal and educational status of Turkish women between 1923 and 1938, under Atatürk's lead-ership, is unmatched by any revolution before or since. Even a short and highly selective list of progressive victories reveals the considerable scope of new rights gained by Turkish women: In 1924, they were granted equal status with men under the new Constitution of the Republic, and the Civil Code, based on the Swiss Civil Code, was established in 1926. In 1930, Turkish women were given the right to vote in local elections, which was expanded in 1934 to include the rights to vote and to be elected in national elections. This all came about decades before similar reforms were made in many current European Union members, including France (1944), Italy (1945), Belgium (1948), Greece (1952) and Portugal (1976). As a result, the first democratic Turkish Parliament in 1950 included 18 female members. Also during the Atatürk era, female heirs gained equal inheritance rights, and gender discrimination in wages was outlawed. Women were granted the full right to own and dispose of property, and were also allowed to enter the army. Polygamy and marriage without the consent of both partners were banned. Both husband and wife could now obtain divorce by applying to a court of law, and the Shariah method of divorce by repudiation was outlawed.

Other revolutionary reforms followed, such as the institution of compulsory and free primary education for all citizens, and newly organized adult literacy classes, which improved the quality of life for Turkish women considerably. Atatürk took an active role in making sure these laws were implemented, and led by example.

During the Independence War, he gave the honorary rank of corporal to Halide Edip Adivar, the first Turkish feminist and his close friend. And, departing from decades of patriarchal tradition, he insisted that his wife, Latife, be present at their own wedding ceremony. At the time, it was unusual for husbands and wives to travel together, but Latife accompanied Atatürk on his official tours of the country. Atatürk also provided all of his adopted children with world-class educations, and his adopted daughters served as models of the modern Turkish women. His adopted daughter Sabiye was a judge, Afet was a history professor and Sabiha Gökçen became an air force pilot at a time when few women were allowed into military forces at all in Europe. During Atatürk's time, Turkish women emerged in the public sphere, working as actresses, enrolling in universities alongside men, even participating in sports. It was Atatürk's leadership that allowed Turkish women to assume powerful professional positions that were previously reserved for men: in 1927 came the first Turkish female lawyer; in 1930 the first female judge and prosecutor in Turkey, and in 1932, the first female diplomat entered the Turkish Foreign Ministry. Turkey even scored an international first, by becoming the first country ever to elect a female judge to the Supreme Court.

European Influences

Due to adopting laws directly from the Swiss Civil Code, there were certain areas where the Turkish Civil Code granted women secondary status. Husbands were officially given head-of-household status, and along with it, the right to withhold permission for their wives to work outside the home. New child guardianship laws also favored the father, who was granted the right to choose the family's place of residence. While this new "family law" had little or no effect on educated, economically advantaged urban women, many of whom were oblivious to it entirely, it rightfully became the focus of feminists' protests in the decades to come.

In the post-Atatürk era, constitutional changes have been sparse, and the socio-economic position of Turkish women has steadily improved, with more and more women entering co-ed universities and achieving positions of influence.

The Turkish feminist steadily grew stronger following the period of relative stagnation during the 1950s and 1960s. Throughout the 1980s and 1990s, groups such as Women's Circle and the Association Against Discrimination of Women actively pursued a feminist consciousness-raising agenda, spearheading petition drives and campaigning against issues such as domestic abuse and sexual harassment. Their efforts culminated in Turkey's signing of the UN [United Nations] Convention on the Elimination of All Kinds of Discrimination against Women (CEDAW) in 1985. During the 1990s, Turkish women's groups brought to national attention and subsequently helped abolish many of the relics of inequality from the Turkish Penal and Civil Codes. In 1990, Article 159 of the Civil Code, which obligated spousal consent for the employment of women, was annulled. In 1993, the Encyclopedia of Women's Associations Worldwide listed 42 active women's organizations in Turkey. That same year, the first Women's Research Department was established at Istanbul University, a postgraduate program was initiated and Turkey elected its first female prime minister. But it wasn't until this past year [2004] the 70th anniversary of Turkish woman's suffrage, that Turkish law was finally fully amended to erase the last vestiges of institutionalized inequality.

On September 1, 2004, the Turkish government incorporated 348 new paragraphs into Turkey's 80-years-old penal code, updating it to match not only European standards, but also the reality of Turkish life in the 21st century. Among other improvements, the new penal code outlaws marital rape and forced virginity tests, and establishes tougher punishments against so-called 'honor killings.' A recent misguided effort to criminalize adultery, widely regarded as an effort to appease the conservative voting public, was defeated under pressure from women's rights groups. Described by Belgian Foreign Minister Karel De Gucht as potentially a 'serious obstacle' to Turkey's bid to join the European Union, the suggested anti-adultery proposition was quickly capitalized upon by parties hostile to Turkish entry as a way to suggest Turkey's essential unfitness. Such responses are typical. European politicians who are antagonistic to the possibility of Turkish membership often make it a point to express doubts about Turkish women's rights. According to Akin Özçer, Turkish Consul

General to Lyon, France, who points out that some French parliamentarians try to characterize secular Turkey as a quasi-Islamic state, using misinformation about Turkey's mainly Muslim population to imply that Turkish women suffer under the yoke of an Islamic patriarchy.

Misperceptions

But in reality, this is merely another version of the burka-covered mermaid: an imaginary hybrid, which, instead of revealing anything about Turkey's gender dynamics, actually unveils French insecurities. To be sure, Turkish women, like women of all nations, do experience discrimination and gender-based hardships in their daily lives. And serious problems like spousal abuse have long been the target of Turkish feminist organizations. Tradition-based 'honor killings,' which, according to feminist scholar Shahrzad Mojab, remain a part of 'Kurdish gender culture,' also deserve the global outcry they have sparked. Yet, despite all these problems, women of Turkey have hardly been veiled mermaids—silent bystanders to injustice. According to Daughters of Atatürk, a Turkish-American women's organization current literacy and professional-employment rates for Turkish women surpass those of any other country in the Middle East, and rival those of Europe and North America. In the competitive fields of architecture, science, medicine, pharmacy and law, at least one out of every three employees is female, and in the technical world of engineering, Turkish female employees are slightly ahead of their American counterparts, with female employees at 12 percent.

Turkey's current laws fully meet European standards, but EU politicians are all too hasty to use even the slightest pretext of discrimination to call into question the country's commitment to these widely popular laws. Perhaps the skeptics should let go of their chimerical [imaginary] mermaids, and instead take a look at the reality of Turkish women's lives, however they are dressed. Turkish women will always make sure their own rights are secure, with or without the European Union, just as they have been doing for over 70 years.

"[The] majority of the women are still not politically, socially and economically equipped for political participation."

Laws Are Not Always Enough to Ensure Women's Voting Rights

Rachel Horner

In the following viewpoint, Rachel Horner analyzes women's voting rights in the West African nation of Sierra Leone. Although women have the right to vote and participate in politics there, argues Horner, a number of factors impedes their political equality and leads many to abstain from voting. In order to overcome tradition, illiteracy and prejudice, several aid groups are endeavoring to improve voter knowledge and participation, Horner says. According to the author, one goal is to elect more women to the local and national legislatures and increase support for a female presidential candidate in the future. Rachel Horner is a journalist who has written extensively about Africa.

As you read, consider the following questions:

1. According to the viewpoint, what are the two primary factors that keep women from voting in Sierra Leone?

2. What is the goal of the nationwide campaign by the 50/50 group, according to the author?

3. What does Horner say the Sierra Leone ballots include in order to accommodate illiterate voters?

Having the right to vote is one thing; using it properly, or indeed at all, is quite another, as Sierra Leone has shown ahead of general elections this Saturday [August 11, 2007].

Almost 50 years have passed since women were first allowed to cast ballots in the West African state. However, some may be prevented from fully exercising their voting rights come Aug. 11 (2007)—in large part because tradition and a lack of education for women keep them excluded from the political process.

Women and Voting

"Women are less likely than men to be able to name the date of the next election, are less likely to be able to name political parties, and are less likely to rate themselves as having a high level of knowledge about the electoral process," notes an overview of key findings from a survey titled 'Sierra Leone Elections 2007: A Comprehensive Baseline Study of Knowledge, Priorities and Trust'.

The study was conducted by the British Broadcasting Corporation (BBC) World Service Trust and Search for Common Ground, an international non-governmental organisation, with funding from Britain's Department for International Development.

While 80 percent of men surveyed said they knew the date of the upcoming vote, 65 percent of women were aware of the

South African Women's Movement Is Failing to Lobby for Women

Despite the fact that over half the 18-million voters in South Africa's [2000] municipal poll [were] women, most parties fared dismally on gender policies. A gender report card, issued by the feminist website, Womensnet, analysed the manifestos of the major parties and awarded not a single A and several Fs.

It indicates that political parties do not yet see the women's vote as an important constituency, but more importantly, it highlights that the women's movement is failing in its lobbying exercises to make politicians see the women's vote as an important bloc to win over.

Farah Khan,
"Gender Policy Widely Ignored in Today's South Africa Election,"
Afrol News, *December 5, 2000,*
www.afrol.com/News/sa017_gender_policy.htm.

date. The percentage of women who knew the date was especially low in Pujehun (52 percent) and Bo (43 percent)—both in eastern Sierra Leone.

Over a third of men claimed to know a lot about the electoral process, compared to a quarter of women surveyed.

Similarly, a 2006 study by the British chapter of aid agency Oxfam and the 50/50 Group found that almost a quarter of persons surveyed in the eastern Kailahun and Koinadugu districts—23.8 percent—believed a woman could not vote for a candidate of her choice.

Helping Women

Efforts are underway to change this situation, however, including a nationwide campaign by the 50/50 Group to ensure greater participation of women in the upcoming presidential and parliamentary polls.

This initiative got underway recently with funding from the African Women's Development Fund, headquartered in Ghana's capital, Accra. The 50/50 Group is a civic organisation that tries to increase women's representation in politics to reflect the fact that they make up about half of the population. Sierra Leone's 2004 census put the country's population at about five million persons, 52 percent of them women.

Addressing journalists in the Sierra Leonean capital of Freetown, Nemata Eshun-Baiden—founder and past president of the group—said the initiative was also aimed at showing women how to avoid casting void ballots.

Notes a 50/50 press release: "Although training (has) been conducted there is a need for more training and awareness-raising of women in breaking the barriers that militate against them participating and making informed choices during elections."

"(The) majority of the women are still not politically, socially and economically equipped for political participation."

The campaign is taking the form of workshops co-led by officials from the National Electoral Commission (NEC). Polling stations are being simulated during these events, to give women the chance to practice voting with the use of mock ballot papers.

Ballots for the election will show pictures of candidates to help illiterate voters—something of particular concern to women in Sierra Leone. According to the 2006 United Nations [U.N.] Development Report, only 24.4 percent of women in the country are literate, compared to 46.9 percent of men.

Other aspects of the voting process are also discussed in the workshops. In addition, messages urging women to vote are being broadcast on radio and television in a number of local languages. According to the survey by the BBC and Search for Common Ground, "A greater proportion of radio listeners than non-listeners know the date of elections, and a greater proportion of listeners than non-listeners report high levels of confidence in their knowledge of the electoral process."

The 50/50 Group plans to work with the electoral commission to assess the effectiveness of the campaign by analysing whether there is a greater turnout of women voters next month, compared to earlier polls (NEC spokesman Isaac Curtis Hooke says about 2.6 million people have registered to vote in the forthcoming elections, 49 percent of them women).

Prospects for Success

But in a country where years of civil war have taken a particular toll on women, are wives and mothers who are consumed by the daily struggle of maintaining households able to attend the workshops?

Eschun-Baiden is optimistic: "We will use megaphones (and) do whatever we can for women to leave their chores to attend our workshops," she told IPS (news).

If women do start to exercise their voting power, they may well change the face of politics in Sierra Leone.

The Oxfam and 50/50 'PACER Baseline Survey Report' found that 75 percent of women interviewed would be willing to vote for a female presidential candidate, while only 55 percent of men were similarly inclined.

Not one of the country's three main political parties has chosen a woman to represent it in the presidential poll.

Women make up 14.5 percent of Sierra Leone's outgoing legislature, and there are also three female cabinet ministers.

Sierra Leone is one of the world's most poverty stricken countries, its extensive diamond reserves having fuelled the brutal civil war that ended in 2002. The U.N. [United Nations] Development Report notes that three quarters of people here live on less than two dollars a day.

Periodical Bibliography

The following articles have been selected to supplement the diverse views presented in this chapter.

Donna Brazile — "Madam Speaker," *Ms.*, Winter 2007.

Mary Chapman and Angela Mills — "Eighty Years and More: Looking Back at the Nineteenth Amendment," *Canadian Review of American Studies*, Winter 2006.

Louisa Dris-Aït-Hamadouche — "Women in the Maghreb: Civil Society's Actors or Political Instruments?" *Middle East Policy*, December 2007.

The Economist — "Gaucho Feminism," December 15, 2007.

Linda Evans — "Locked Up, Then Locked Out: Women Coming Out of Prison," *Women & Therapy*, Fall 2006.

Deepa Kandsawmi — "Kuwait Taps Women," *Herizons*, Fall 2005.

Aie-Rie Lee and Mikyung Chin — "The Women's Movement in South Korea," *Social Science Quarterly*, December 2007.

Nancy MacLean — "Gender Is Powerful: The Long Reach of Feminism," *OAH Magazine of History*, October 2006.

Bill Marsh — "Women Gain Votes (Some Even Matter)," *New York Times*, May 22, 2005.

Helen Rizzo, Abdel-Hamid Abdel-Latif, Katherine Meyer — "The Relationship Between Gender Equality and Democracy: A Comparison of Arab Versus Non-Arab Muslim Societies," *Sociology*, December 2007.

Wendy Smooth — "Intersectionality in Electoral Politics: A Mess Worth Making," *Politics Gender*, September 2006.

Pamela Stumpo — "Egypt as a Woman: Nationalism, Gender and Politics," *International Journal of Middle East Studies*, November 2007.

OPPOSING
VIEWPOINTS®
SERIES

CHAPTER 4

How Should Global Voting Rights Be Expanded?

Chapter Preface

Politicians and officials around the world have endeavored to expand voting rights as part of broader initiatives to get more people to vote and therefore participate in the political process. Voting is seen as the best way to promote democracy and equality. It also serves to ensure that policies reflect the will of the people. Lyndon B. Johnson, the thirty-sixth president of the United States, once stated that "the vote is the most powerful instrument ever devised by man for breaking down injustice and destroying the terrible walls which imprison men because they are different from other men."

There is considerable debate over the best way to increase voting rights. One method that has been tested is e-voting. E-voting, or electronic voting, emerged out of concerns over the complexity of ballots and the accuracy of ballot counting. Proponents believe that touch-screen voting machines could simplify voting procedures and people would not have to worry about whether their vote was fairly counted. However, concerns over e-voting have arisen, including fears that the machines could be manipulated by hackers. Along with concerns over the accuracy of voting methods, concerns have also arisen regarding the integrity of government systems in providing all citizens with their due voting rights. They maintain that corruption and repression in some countries can prevent the fair spread of voting rights. Those concerned with allowing increased voter participation have also suggested that governments lower the legal voting age to sixteen years of age. Whereas most countries currently allow people to vote at eighteen, some restrict the right to vote to as late as twenty-one or older. Proponents of lowering the voting age to sixteen point to the success of the policy in countries such as Austria, Brazil, Cuba, and Nicaragua. However, opponents argue that sixteen-year-olds are not mature enough to vote. They also point out that younger citizens do not pay taxes and are often not able to marry, own property, or join the military and therefore they should not be able to make decisions on these issues.

The viewpoints in this chapter examine e-voting, government influence over voting rights, and lowering the voting age. The authors of the following essays explore the best way to spread voting rights while maintaining equality and ensuring the fairness of the ballot process.

> *"The idea of voting in public elections over the Internet can be seen as a logical extension of Internet applications in commerce and government."*

E-Voting Can Benefit the Voting Process

Jörgen Svensson and Ronald Leenes

In the following viewpoint, Jörgen Svensson and Ronald Leenes examine the prospects of e-voting, or electronic voting, as a means to enhance suffrage and perpetuate voting rights. Specifically, the authors explore e-voting in three countries, the United Kingdom, Switzerland, and the Netherlands. E-voting is seen as a way to increase participation in elections and to improve efficiency in vote tabulations, state Svensson and Leenes, but each country's societal and political characteristics should be considered before an e-voting method is adopted. Jörgen Svensson and Ronald Leenes are both at the University of Twente in the Netherlands and have done extensive research on e-voting.

As you read, consider the following questions:

1. According to the viewpoint, what are the main reasons the United Kingdom is promoting e-voting?

2. What do Svensson and Leenes say Switzerland already has introduced to increase voter turnout?

3. What, according to the authors, is the connection between e-voting and electronic identification systems?

Many people routinely undertake electronic transactions and some cast their votes in polls on Internet sites and contests on television. The idea of voting in public elections over the Internet can be seen as a logical extension of Internet applications in commerce and government. E-voting and e-participation are appearing on the political agenda and experiments are held in various places. Judging from reports in the popular media and claims by enthusiastic proponents, the prospects of electronic voting are excellent. There are, however, also more cautious voices. They draw attention to the problems e-voting may cause with respect to fundamental principles underlying the voting process. Voting may be more than just another government service that can be improved by ICT [Information and Communication Technology].

The E-voting Debate

In the debate, arguments in favour or against e-voting are often presented as objective and fixed and they are used by both sides to make definite claims about the desired measures to be taken, irrespective of the particular social context.

In this paper we argue that deciding on the adoption of e-voting is not a simple matter of evaluating objective benefits and threats and selecting the one and only optimal strategy. Instead, differences in social context matter. Countries, populations, electoral systems, public attitudes, political and administrative arrangements vary widely and all these factors play a role in assessing the merits of e-voting in a particular context. This means that in different countries with different institutional contexts the decisions on whether or not to introduce a particular kind of e-voting are structured in different ways, and may lead to very different outcomes....

Different Form of E-voting

E-voting is generally seen as any type of voting that involves electronic means. Although e-voting can be conceived in many different ways, a crucial distinction may be made between electronic machine voting (eMV) and electronic distance voting (eDV). eMV simply refers to the use of any electronic apparatus to record and count votes in a fixed public place. This may be a specialised voting machine in a voting booth or a stand-alone PC [personal computer] specially installed for this purpose in a voting kiosk.

eDV goes a step further in the sense that it implies the electronic registration, culling and counting of votes cast from different locations. It typically allows the voter to use a more generic technology such as interactive digital TV, telephone, Short Message Service (SMS) or the Internet, to cast his vote from any preferred place, be it from the home or the office or even from a deck chair on a cruise ship somewhere in the Caribbean.

Both eMV, and especially eDV, are considered to provide new opportunities for the organisation of elections.

eMV may be especially helpful for a reliable, objective, efficient and expeditious counting of the votes and may also offer some possibilities for electronic verification (e.g., the verification whether the user is indeed entitled to vote and whether the vote is cast correctly).

Although eDV may also be expected to offer these benefits, its particular strength is that it enables people to vote without having to go to a special polling station. It thus provides the prospect of reducing the effort to vote, especially for people who find it difficult to visit a polling station on election day, such as the physically challenged, or people living in remote areas.

As proponents of e-voting point out, these possibilities of eMV and eDV may help to make voting more cost effective and easier and to increase voter turnout. Especially when eDV is used as part of a multi-channel approach and a combination of different forms of voting is offered, voters have an option to vote by the means they prefer.

Finally, e-voting is considered to be a way to modernise the voting process and to give voting a new, modern, image. According to some commentators, modern people and especially young voters are used to the idea of electronic transactions and simply expect government to provide the possibility of electronic voting. . . .

The United Kingdom

In order to explain the e-voting ambitions in the United Kingdom [UK], we find that we can point at several reasons why this country is more eager to adopt e-voting than others.

First of all, an important factor to consider is the strong modernization drive within the UK government. Many policy documents all over the world express the desire to modernise government and to invest in becoming an e-society, with of course, an e-Government. However, where most of them mainly produce e-government rhetoric, the UK seems to take e-government serious, by establishing agencies such as the office of the e-Envoy and the fact that e-government is the responsibility of a senior Cabinet member. Modernising the voting process to bring it up to 21st century lifestyles is an endeavour that fits the e-governments' general aims.

Secondly, an important factor in explaining the British interest in eDV is the serious decline in voter turnout, which is seen as a major cause of concern. The consultation paper on e-democracy produced by the e-Envoy lists the following figures:

- Turnout in the 2001 General Election was 59%—a fall of 12% from the 1997 figure and the lowest since 1918.

- Approximately 60% of 18–24 year olds did not vote in the 2001 General Election.

- In the UK, only 24% turned out to vote in the 1999 European parliamentary election, compared to 37% in 1994.

- Turnout in the 2002 local elections was 35%.

Related to the problem of decreasing turnout, the Political Parties, Elections and Referendums Act 2000 (PPERA) has been enacted. This act has established the Electoral Commission, whose principal aims include the encouragement of participation in the democratic process, and increase levels of electoral registration and voting. Where the concerns about low turnout already led to the introduction of postal ballots, we may see the introduction of ICT as an additional measure along this line. Although both the e-Envoy and the Electoral commission stress that the introduction of postal ballots and ICT in itself will not increase voter turnout, the decreasing turnout is still an important factor driving the e-voting enthusiasm.

Moreover, as the PPERA allows local authorities to conduct pilots with new voting techniques under supervision of the Electoral Commission, it has opened the door for many local entrepreneurs who may be eager to have a go at e-voting, for many different reasons. Not only are the local experiments seen as an excellent chance for local authorities to promote themselves as modern and efficient, also several local managers seem to regard e-voting as an excellent career opportunity. In this enthusiasm local authorities and their managers find themselves backed by international 'election service providers', who according to [J.] Ledbetter "spend like mad" to ensure that such elections work and the whole world will hear about them.

E-Voting Success in India and Venezuela

India, whose per-capita income is a 70th that of the United States, has moved to an electronic system that ties a million terminals together to enable the entire country's citizens to vote digitally. In India's most recent elections, e-voting machines counted every ballot. Nearly 390 million people voted out of a possible 670 million eligible to vote, according to data from the Election Commission of India.

Venezuela has also converted its ballot boxes to digital devices. In the recent attempt to recall President Chavez, nearly 70 percent of the voters, or about 10 million people, turned out to cast their votes on touch-screen terminals, according to the Consejo Nacional Electoral, Venezuela's electoral council.

Robert Lemos, "Global Lessons in E-Voting,"
CNet News, September 30, 2004,
www.news.com/Global-lessons-in-e-voting
/2009-1008_3-5387540.html.

Switzerland

With respect to Switzerland we also see related reasons that may explain enthusiasm with respect to eDV.

Switzerland, just like the UK has an important turnout problem, especially for the national parliamentary elections (43.22% for the 1999 elections, slightly down from 1995). In order to make elections easier and increase turnout, Switzerland already introduced postal voting which is fairly popular. E-voting is seen as a logical extension to postal voting, that can help increase voter turnout, although also in Switzerland there is skepticism about the effect of e-voting on turnout.

In addition to this, [H.] Geser lists four other arguments why the Swiss political system is especially prone to e-voting:

- The extreme large number of polling procedures (elections as well as issue votings) on the federal, cantonal and communal level that take place each year implies that e-voting may lead to considerable economic and organisational advantages;

- Voter registration procedures in Switzerland are on a very high level, contrary to the voter registration on the local level in many other countries, which may facilitate the introduction of e-voting;

- By adopting postal vote laws in the 1990s, Switzerland has already gone a long way towards "distant-polling" and so the Swiss are no longer required to appear at the polling station and polling has already become "desacralized".

- The introduction of e-voting is facilitated, because norms concerning the secrecy of votes are less pronounced than in many other Western Countries. This due to a long tradition of public votings, where voting takes place by counting raised hands.

The Netherlands

Finally, the Netherlands. In a sense, the Netherlands seems to be the odd one out.

On the one hand, the weight of the most crucial arguments in favour of introducing eDV seems limited here. Voter turnout decreased over the last decades, but not as dramatically as in the UK or in Switzerland (in the last, turbulent elections of 2002 there was in fact a slight increase). As the Netherlands is the most densely populated country in Europe, organising access to polling stations has never been a major problem. In most municipalities eMV is in place, which means that the elections are run very efficiently, with some of the smaller municipalities capable of offering the tabulated votes seconds after the polls close.

On the other hand, when we look at the arguments against eDV, the Netherlands has a history of being prudent in protecting the individual and promoting the secret character of voting. For this reason, postal voting never made it in the Netherlands and proxy voting is limited (a voter may cast a maximum of two proxy votes). So, when we look at these arguments, we would not really expect the Netherlands to be among the forerunners in the field.

When we really have to explain why the Dutch seem to be taking the road to eDV we are left with two types of structuration arguments.

The first one is that the very extensive and positive experience with eMV may have something to do with it. As far as we know, the Dutch have the longest experience with electronic machine voting in the world and thus are really used to the application of this technology in the voting process. This may be a reason why policy makers in the Netherlands are less fearful about eDV than policy makers in other countries.

The second type of argument has to do with political ambitions and political lobbying. Just like the British, the Dutch government tries to be at the forefront of e-government and just like in Britain, there are some direct links between the development of e-government and the development of e-voting. Not only are both developments furthered by the same responsible ministry, the introduction of e-voting is also seen as one of the best chances for introducing a nation wide electronic identification system, which in the Netherlands is considered a difficult, but essential step in the further development of e-Government service delivery.

Moreover, the new former minister for e-government who was one of the driving forces behind e-voting, is a member of D66, a party that has campaigned for the introduction of referendums and elected majors since its reception in 1966, an aim which really fits the promises of e-voting. Thirdly, there is an active e-voting lobby consisting of organizations such as PELS (the Platform ELectronic voting) and EPN (Electronic Highway Platform NL), which has been successful in mobilizing politicians to back e-voting. This has resulted in persistent demand from members of parliament to continue with the introduction of e-voting.

> "We found a system so vulnerable in it-
> self that you didn't need to put mali-
> cious code into it to rig an election."

E-Voting Is Flawed

Kim Zetter

*Kim Zetter in the following viewpoint analyzes problems with
equipment used for e-voting, or electronic voting, specifically
Diebold machines that are commonly used in the United States.
Zetter highlights how researchers discovered problems with voting machines and reported the issues to the press and government officials, but the manufacturers of the devices resisted calls
for improvements. The author suggests ways to improve the security of the machines. Kim Zetter is a freelance journalist in Oak-
land, California, who frequently writes for* Wired, *a magazine
and Web site that reports on trends.*

As you read, consider the following questions:

1. According to the author, what was the major problem
   with the key to the encryption of the Diebold e-voting
   machines?
2. In what year were problems with Diebold's encryption
   key first discovered, according to the viewpoint?

3. What does Zetter say is the Mercuri Method?

In 1997, the Costa Rican government asked AT&T Labs Research, where [Avi] Rubin was working, to design an e-voting system. But after Rubin met with them, "they decided we had scared them sufficiently about security and scrapped the whole project," he said.

Rubin was also a panelist for an e-voting feasibility study launched by the National Science Foundation at the request of President [Bill] Clinton in 2000. And he had just finished teaching a graduate course on e-voting security in which students spent the first weeks of the class designing e-voting systems, then devising ways to break into them.

"No system in the class was unbreakable," Rubin said. "It was really good training for the Diebold [voting machine] thing."

Research on E-voting

He contacted two grad students, 25-year-old Yoshi Kohno, a University of California at San Diego student who was in Maryland for the summer, and 22-year-old Adam Stubblefield, who was only two years away from completing his Ph.D. at Johns Hopkins.

Stubblefield made a name for himself in 2001 when he and a team of researchers that included Rubin cracked the encryption code used in Wi-Fi networks and exposed the networks' insecurity. The news made headlines and led the industry to revamp the wireless encryption protocol. He was also part of a group that broke the music industry's watermark code, which had been designed to thwart piracy.

Rubin told the students he had a "drop everything" project. By the time the three convened, Stubblefield had already downloaded the Diebold code and printed it out.

He and Kohno divvied up reams of paper and attacked the code with highlighters and pens. Within half an hour they discovered the first serious flaw.

Vote Counts, cartoon by Breen. ©2006, Copley News Service.

E-Voting Problems

It was a basic error that students in Cryptography 101 learn never to make: Diebold's programmers had written the key for unscrambling the system's encryption directly into the code. This meant the key would never change, and anyone reading the source code (including anyone who downloaded it from the FTP [file transfer protocol] site) would know it. The same key unlocked the data on every machine. It was the equivalent of a bank assigning the same PIN to every customer's ATM [automated teller machine] card.

"Oh man, we thought, this is horrible," said Kohno. "We realized that the system was written by novices and we weren't really surprised then by anything else we found."

For two weeks they did little but pore over the code and write their analysis. They talked to no one about what they were doing, fearing that Diebold would try to stop them with a restraining order.

Initially, they thought they might find malicious code in the software that would allow the results of elections to be changed at will. Computer scientists had long contended that anyone with access to a voting system could slip the code in and no one would know.

"We found a system that was so vulnerable in itself that you didn't need to put malicious code into it to rig an election," Kohno said. The system, they concluded, was open to attack from both inside and out.

In July 2003, they released a 23-page report. . . .

The timing was critical because Rubin's own state, Maryland, had just signed a $56 million contract to purchase Diebold machines. Georgia had used 22,000 of the machines exclusively in its 2002 gubernatorial election, and California was well on its way to purchasing thousands of them.

"There was only a fixed amount of time until the next primaries to get the machines secure," Rubin said.

None of them could have predicted the publicity that ensued. TV crews lined the hall outside Rubin's office, and the three spent the next several days doing nonstop interviews. Rubin went to Capitol Hill to brief congressional staff and then testified before the Maryland legislature. He was named a Baltimorean of the year by *Baltimore* magazine, even though he'd only moved to the city a year earlier.

Diebold

David Jefferson, a computer scientist at Lawrence Livermore National Laboratory who served on California's e-voting task force with Stanford [University] computer scientist [David L.] Dill, called the report "a watershed event" that showed things were "far worse than any of us had ever dreamed."

"It's one thing for a computer scientist to say we know what the security issues are, but you can only go so far without having the hard evidence," Jefferson said. "Avi and his authors were the first to get the hard evidence. I think it was a thunderclap to the security and election communities."

Diebold derided the report as an amateurish "homework assignment" by grad students and said the researchers had examined old code that was never used in an election, a claim that was later disproved. Election officials accused the Johns Hopkins team of courting media attention and recklessly undermining the public's confidence in elections. Rubin said that other critics even sent a letter to the president of Johns Hopkins [University] trying to get him fired.

"We weren't concerned about being refuted," Stubblefield said. "We knew the technical accuracy of what we discovered. (Critics) could try to spin things against us, but in the end truth prevails."

It wasn't the first time someone had found problems with Diebold's system. Doug Jones, a computer scientist at the University of Iowa and a member of Iowa's voting system board of examiners, found the same problems in 1997 when his state was considering buying the systems. Jones was particularly disturbed by the same problem that Kohno and Stubblefield found regarding the encryption key that was coded into the system and was the same for every voting machine. He told Diebold about his finding, but a non-disclosure agreement prevented him from going public.

"I was disappointed to see that the company had done nothing to fix the problems in all of these years," Jones said after reading the Johns Hopkins report. Diebold spokesman David Bear said the company fixed the encryption key problem after a second research report came out last September [2003] that raised the same concerns raised by Doug Jones and Rubin's group.

"If any of the multitudes of reviewers of our system find any issues we immediately investigate the issues and where appropriate modify the system to address the issues," Bear wrote in an e-mail.

Early Warnings

Long before Jones expressed his concerns about the Diebold system, computer scientist Rebecca Mercuri, an e-voting expert and a fellow at Harvard University's Kennedy School of Government, had been warning about the insecurity of e-voting in general ever since her Pennsylvania county contemplated buying e-voting equipment in 1989. She helped convince New York City to abandon a planned $60 million voting contract with Sequoia, but few others, including computer scientists, took her warnings seriously.

Although any voting system is open to fraud, digital machines made it easier to affect vast numbers of votes with little effort, Mercuri said. She was the first to call for voter-verified paper ballots to be used with e-voting machines. The Mercuri Method, as it's now known, would require machines to produce a paper receipt that voters could see, but not touch, to verify that the machine recorded their votes correctly before the receipt is deposited into a secure ballot box. It's a solution that nearly all critics of e-voting are now demanding.

> *"The Liberian people had an opportunity to elect new leadership . . . and people voted for freedom; they voted to have a voice in their government."*

Foreign Governments Are Needed to Help Spread Democracy in Other Countries

Jendayi E. Frazer

In this viewpoint, Jendayi E. Frazer details how governments can spread democracy and improve voting rights through aid and technical assistance. The viewpoint concentrates on U.S. efforts to assist Liberia in the early 2000s that resulted in the election of Ellen Johnson Sirleaf, the first democratically elected woman president in Africa. Frazer also highlights past American influence in the country and argues that a combination of aid and diplomatic pressure is necessary to promote voter rights and ensure free and fair elections. Jendayi E. Frazer is the assistant secretary for African Affairs for the United States Department of State.

Jendayi E. Frazer, "Remarks to the Subcommittee on Africa, Global Human Rights and International Operations," U.S. Department of State, House International Relations Committee, February 8, 2006. Accessed online at www.state.gov/p/af/rls/rm/2006/61150.htm.

As you read, consider the following questions:

1. According to the viewpoint, what nearby countries have been impacted by Liberia's internal conflict? How will democracy in Liberia encourage stability in the war-torn region?

2. How long does Frazer say the civil war lasted in Liberia?

3. How much money does Liberia owe the U.S. government, according to the author?

We are living in a period of unique opportunity for Africa. Across the continent, civil conflicts are giving way to civil society and free elections. The election and inauguration of Liberia's new president, Ellen Johnson Sirleaf, is a prime example. This is a nation with whom the United States has historically shared a close relationship. This is also a nation whose development and productivity were hobbled for 14 years by civil war. But now, Liberia has given the African continent its first democratically elected woman president. Changes are underway, and there are many reasons to be hopeful for the Liberian people and their neighbors.

While working with our African partners, I am always cognizant of President [George W.] Bush's directive to make the world "safer, better, and freer." This phrase encapsulates the President's foreign policy objectives. President Bush supports policies that involve making real changes in the lives of real people, and this Administration's policies on Liberia are one noteworthy piece of the larger picture being painted by Members of Congress and professional staff at various federal agencies.

This is a good news story about Americans supporting African efforts to better Africa. As Secretary [of State Condoleezza] Rice recently noted, "Transformational diplomacy is rooted in partnership, not paternalism; in doing things with other people, not for them. We seek to use America's diplomatic power to help foreign citizens to better their own lives and to build their own nations and to transform their own futures.". . .

Regional Stability

President Bush's strategy for national defense is one of global peace and security. In practice, this means working bilaterally or multilaterally to address given situations. It means working with regional and sub-regional organizations, such as the African Union and Mano River Union. Since 2001, one of the central elements of President Bush's Africa policy has been the emphasis on supporting the capacity of African countries and regional organizations to mediate conflicts and carry out peacekeeping operations, to reduce the amount of external help that is needed.

The President understands that regional conflicts have global repercussions. Consider the fact of civilian deaths, refugees and internally displaced persons, arable land that lies uncultivated, and stagnant economies that offer parents no way to support their children. Liberia's internal conflict produced untold death and destruction, shattered the nation's infrastructure, and exported trouble to nearby states, such as Sierra Leone and Guinea.

Liberia's former president Charles Taylor bears much of the responsibility for Liberia's suffering. The U.S. Government has consistently maintained that Taylor must be brought to justice before the Special Court. This will significantly help to bring closure to a tragic chapter in Liberia's history and help all of West Africa overcome patterns of impunity, illicit trade, and civil conflict.

Liberia's condition is clearly of concern beyond its own borders. If Liberia is internally secure, all of West Africa will benefit. It becomes easier for the region to address the ongoing unrest in Côte d'Ivoire, as well as fragile situations in Guinea and Sierra Leone. A stable Liberia is a force for regional stability.

With few interludes, Liberia's civil war raged for 14 years. In the spring and summer of 2003, President Bush supported the Economic Community of West African States (ECOWAS) in putting together a comprehensive agreement toward a lasting peace. When chaos broke out in the streets of the capital, President Bush sent U.S. Marines into Liberia to protect the innocent and create a sense of order amid the chaos. Only Nigerian soldiers arrived earlier than our Marines.

The American action was historic, and represented the first time American boots had touched African soil for stability operations in nearly a decade. Following that deployment, the United States stayed the course in Liberia with further logistical assistance to the ECOWAS Mission in Liberia (ECOMIL) and provided extensive humanitarian assistance. On September 19, 2003, the United Nations Security Council adopted Resolution 1509, which established a peacekeeping operation in Liberia, known as UNMIL [United Nations Mission in Liberia]. UNMIL consists of 15,000 troops plus a sizeable contingent of UN police officers and military observers. This force has helped maintain calm.

The Liberians agreed among themselves on a transitional government that paved the way for free and fair elections in October 2005. National reconstruction is underway, and the United States has taken the lead as the major contributor. The U.S. Congress generously appropriated over $880 million in the last two fiscal years to help with reconstruction efforts. More than $520 million of that money has supported UNMIL. For fiscal year 2006, we have allocated more than $270 million for continued support of the nation's reconstruction and peacekeeping efforts.

Liberia continues to benefit from various U.S. Government funding, including: Economic Support Funds, Development

Assistance, Migration and Refugee Assistance, P.L. 480 Title II food aid, and Child Survival Health Funds. The United States has the largest diplomatic mission in Liberia, and the United States is supporting security reforms, including the new Liberian National Police Academy. Between 2004 and 2005, the United States contributed $60 million to support the training and equipping of a civilian-led Liberian military force. Recruiting for the new army began on January 18 [2007], and the goal is to have a new army of 2,000 soldiers ready by 2008.

Sending American Marines into Monrovia was a bold action with positive results. After years of turmoil, Liberians are beginning a long process of reconstruction and post-war recovery. Nearly two decades of conflict left the national infrastructure in shambles and left people without basic services, such as access to clean water and electricity. A generation of children has only known war and destruction. They are now looking to a peaceful and democratic nation to meet their hopes for a future of dignity and an opportunity to support themselves.

The tide has turned, and since 2003, Liberians have had the opportunity to restore order, create a responsive government, and welcome refugees home. Liberia's transition from war to peace is a crucial and historic development. As former General and President Dwight Eisenhower noted many years ago, "We seek peace, knowing that peace is the climate of freedom." That remains true. Today, we seek peace by sowing seeds of democracy.

Democratization

The United States has had a close relationship with Liberia dating back to the 1820s. In fact, the United States and Liberia have been close allies, particularly throughout the Cold War and up until civil war broke out in 1989. As we look to the future, there is reason to believe we can renew that close friendship.

The Liberian people had an opportunity to elect new leadership [in 2005] and people voted for freedom; they voted to have a voice in their national government. The U.S. government policy is to support and encourage democratic rule abroad, and for that reason, the United States spent $10 million in support of last October's [2007] election. We believe that freedom is the way forward. Every nation's government will reflect local cultures and values, but only a free government can hope to protect individuals' liberty and nurture its people's untapped potential.

In Liberia, our goal is to support local efforts to stand up a freely elected government, a dynamic economy, and the health, educational, and other services that are essential to the well-being of any nation. The peaceful and fair election of Ellen Johnson Sirleaf is encouraging. Her win symbolizes a victory for gender inclusiveness.

We have made great progress since 2003 due to the concerted effort of the many American public servants who were mobilized to engage on so many levels. Our Congress, the Department of Defense, the Department of Treasury, the Marines, USAID [United States Aid for International Development], and the State Department all helped to effect this transition. At the American Embassy in Monrovia, our diplomats have done an extraordinary service over the last two and a half years in helping Liberians move past the era of civil war and toward a better future. This is a Liberian solution to a Liberian challenge. Americans are participating, but only as partners.

The United States continues to support Liberian recovery efforts as an important element of our security, political, economic, and humanitarian strategy for West Africa. After all, nations with democratically elected governments can resolve internal disputes on Election Day, and they are unlikely to destabilize or terrorize their own people or adjacent nations.

Toward this end, we have and will continue to offer monetary and other assistance. The U.S. government has proactively engaged the international community and advocated on behalf of Liberia. In February 2004, this country co-hosted an international conference on Liberia's reconstruction. Donors pledged more than $522 million in assistance. The United States contributed $200 million toward the critical humanitarian needs of refugees and displaced persons, community revitalization, independent media, policing, social services, and other sectors.

In fiscal years 2004 and 2005, the United States contributed $520 million to the UN [United Nations] Mission in Liberia and $75 million for community reintegration, including work and education programs for youths and former combatants. Another $23 million has supported the rule of law, including judicial structures and civilian police programs.

The United States continues to support these indispensable programs. After years of civil war, the physical infrastructure needs to be rebuilt from the ground up, but in many cases, so does the social network. Almost half of Liberia's 3.3 million people were uprooted during the civil war, and some 190,000 Liberians remain in other countries, including Côte d'Ivoire, Ghana, Guinea, and Sierra Leone. Interpersonal relationships and reconciliation, as well as coming to terms with the atrocities committed during the civil war, are part of the new government's agenda.

The U.S. government has funded a program in support of law and justice that will send a resident legal advisor and a five-person team of technical experts to Liberia. This team will help improve the Liberian criminal justice system. We will help launch a Truth and Reconciliation Commission, while also supporting an access to justice program to increase the confidence of Liberians to resolve disputes efficiently, fairly and effectively through the justice sector. Additionally, we will work to establish legal advice centers and a national referral network; integrate alternative dispute mechanisms; and provide incentives to attract public defenders.

President Bush intends to remain engaged with Liberia, while this restored democracy finds its footing. For that reason, the Administration plans to allocate nearly $43 million in fiscal year 2006 Economic Support Fund (ESF) money, including some $6 million to be made available immediately for quick-impact projects, including rebuilding schools, court houses, and hospitals. Roads that connect Liberia's major cities also need to be built. All in all, including planned allocations for the current fiscal year, the United States' contribution to Liberia's reconstruction for fiscal years 2004–2006 will exceed $1 billion. Our financial contributions underscore the seriousness of our commitment to Liberia's future. President Bush, members of his Administration, and members of Congress agree—we are all dedicated to helping Liberia realize its tremendous promise.

Economic Prosperity

Direct aid is helpful, but it is by no means a panacea [cure-all]. As Secretary Rice recently remarked, "America's foreign assistance must promote responsible sovereignty, not permanent dependency." It is with those words in mind that we move to the third point—the importance of promoting economic prosperity and security.

Liberia has the potential to be a regional economic force. It has valuable natural resources, which could be exported abroad; this would create many local jobs and generate revenue to finance the nation's budget. Before its civil war, Liberia was a major exporter of iron ore and natural rubber. The country is rich in diamonds, gold and other minerals as well as natural resources such as timber and agriculture that are additional sources of potential economic activity. However,

U.S. Support for Democracy in Burma

In the last few weeks [October 2007], the world has been inspired by the courage of the Burmese people. Ordinary men and women have taken to the streets in peaceful marches to demand their freedom and call for democratic change. The world has also been horrified by the response of Burma's military junta. Monks have been beaten and killed. Thousands of pro-democracy protestors have been arrested. . . .

Burma's rulers continue to defy the world's just demands to stop their vicious persecution. They continue to dismiss calls to begin peaceful dialogue aimed at national reconciliation. Most of all, they continue to reject the clear will of the Burmese people to live in freedom under leaders of their own choosing.

George W. Bush,
"President Bush Discusses Sanctions on Burma,"
Press Release, October 19, 2007, www.whitehouse.gov/
news/releases/2007/10/print/20071017-11.html.

much investment will be required to restore these industries and Liberia's dilapidated infrastructure.

Spurring widespread economic growth poses both short-term and long-term challenges for the new Liberian government. Since Liberia's prolonged crisis was in large part financed by illegal sales of the nation's major natural commodities, the UN passed Resolution 1343 in 2001 to forbid the import of Liberian diamonds by any member countries. Another resolution forbidding the import of Liberian timber followed in 2003. With timber products under UN sanction, the Liberian government's main source of income in recent years has been maritime revenue (approximately $13.5 million in 2004) and import taxes (roughly $23 million in 2004).

The new Liberian government is expected to encourage the UN to lift these sanctions and prod the growth of export-oriented jobs within Liberia. Toward this end, Liberia must move quickly and aggressively to address the concerns underlying those sanctions. The United States is working with the Liberian government through the Liberia Forest Initiative (LFI) to establish transparency and effective management in the forest sector and to fortify the government's oversight of this important sector. In a similar fashion, the United States is working with the international community to bring better governance and transparency to Liberia's diamond export industry.

In addition to sector-specific work, the U.S. government is involved with macro economic policy assistance to the country. The United States is a driving force behind the well regarded Governance and Economic Management Assistance Program (GEMAP). GEMAP is intended to reduce corruption, improve revenue collection and increase expenditure transparency, thereby channeling Liberia's revenue-generating resources into efficient and effective uses by the Liberian government. The international financial institutions (IFis) will be tracking Liberia's progress for improved economic management and consistent implementation of the GEMAP program before considering normalizing relations, addressing IFI arrears of $1.4 billion, providing new assistance, and eventual debt relief. Liberia carries a heavy bilateral debt burden, as well. Bilateral creditors, owed $763 million year-end 2004, will also be looking to the new government's economic management performance before initiating debt relief. Liberia owes $382 million to the U.S. Government alone.

This might seem an insurmountable obstacle, but there is good reason to believe that with a significant track record of performance Ellen Johnson Sirleaf and her government will be able to reach agreement with the World Bank, the IMF [International Monetary Fund], and others for alleviation of her nation's massive debt burden. The U.S. plans to work closely with Liberia and its creditors to help resolve the debt situation.

The U.S. Treasury Department's Office of Technical Assistance has been heavily engaged in Liberia, providing assistance on budget and debt management, banking supervision, and tax collection systems. There are currently two resident advisors, one in the Bureau of the Budget and one in the Central Bank. The budget engagement has focused on building capacity within the Bureau of the Budget, so that the Ministry of Finance can better formulate and execute the budget. The banking supervision program has focused on building capacity within the banking supervision department to improve its ability to properly regulate and oversee the banking sector. The tax project is a comprehensive plan involving technical assistance, as well as hardware and software, in an effort to stem corruption and increase revenue flows to the newly elected government.

"[Some autocrats] are trying to redefine democracy and dumb it down."

The Spread of Democracy Requires More than the Right to Vote

Peter Grier

In the viewpoint that follows, Peter Grier details the challenges to the spread of democracy, including the rise of alternative systems of government. Since the 1990s, the number of democratic governments in the world has remained stable, he reports, and some previously democratic governments have undertaken actions that have undermined freedom. Grier further notes that repressive states have used oil revenues to provide services and benefits to their citizenry, thereby reducing demands for democracy. The result is that nondemocratic regimes have been able to offer substitute systems of government to the world. Peter Grier is a journalist for the Christian Science Monitor.

As you read, consider the following questions:

1. According to Grier, how many countries does Freedom House rate as "fully free"?

Peter Grier, "Global Spread of Democracy Stalled," *Christian Science Monitor*, November 21, 2007. Copyright © 2007 The Christian Science Publishing Society. All rights reserved. Reproduced by permission from *Christian Science Monitor (www.csmonitor .com)*. Accessed online at www.csmonitor.com/2007/1121/p01s02-usgn.html?page=1.

2. What nondemocratic governments are using oil revenues to prevent democratization, as mentioned in the viewpoint?

3. According to the author, what countries have presented themselves as "alternatives" to Western ideals of democracy?

The spread of democracy has been one of the defining geopolitical trends of the last 25 years. In 1975, 30 nations of the world had popularly elected governments. By 2005 that number had rocketed to 119.

But in recent years the growth of democracy and political freedom has slowed. In a number of countries—such as Venezuela and some of the former Soviet states—it's even begun to slip backward.

Challenges to Democracy

And for the first time since the heyday of communism, democracy may be facing competition from an ideology that styles itself as an alternative. Enriched by oil money, autocrats such as Vladimir Putin of Russia and Venezuela's Hugo Chávez are challenging the importance of checks on executive power, the rule of law, and unfettered media.

"They are trying to redefine democracy and dumb it down," says Thomas Melia, deputy executive director of Freedom House, a think tank that promotes democracy and rates the performance of governments around the world.

First, the good news. The days when the United States and the Soviet Union seemed locked in a great wrestling match over the ideological fate of the world are long gone. After the collapse of Soviet-style communism as a competitive alternative to representational government, popular votes became the norm in much of the globe.

Historians of the future may judge this to be the era of democracy's triumph.

"In the last quarter of the twentieth century this form of government enjoyed a remarkable rise. Once confined to a handful of wealthy countries, it became, in a short period of time, the most popular political system in the world," writes Michael Mandelbaum, a professor at the Johns Hopkins School of Advanced International Studies, in the current issue of the journal *Foreign Affairs*.

What we know as democracy today is really the fusion of two things, notes Mandelbaum: popular sovereignty, or voting; and individual liberty or freedom. It's easy to hold a national referendum, but establishing liberty is much more difficult, as it requires laws, police, legislatures, and other institutional trappings of freedom.

In its most recent annual survey, Freedom House rates 90 countries in the world as fully free, meaning they are democracies with established liberties. Fifty-eight are partly free, and 45 are not free, according to Freedom House.

Democracy Signed

The percentage of nations rated free has not gone up for a decade. And in Asia, the Middle East, Africa, and the territory of the former Soviet Union, once-promising democratic transitions have turned out to be shallowly rooted.

"There has been a fairly long-term process of stagnation in democracy . . . and now we're seeing individual bits of bad news," says Thomas Carothers, vice president for studies, international politics, and governance, at the Carnegie Endowment for International Peace.

In Pakistan, President Pervez Musharra has begun freeing thousands of opponents from jails across the country, but his declaration of emergency rule has enraged opposition lawyers and set the country's political cauldron on full boil.

In Venezuela, President Hugo Chávez, elected to a six-year term with 60 percent of the vote in 2000, is pushing forward

The Pushback Against Democracy

One of the most troubling developments identified is a growing "pushback" against organizations, movements, and media that monitor human rights or advocate for the expansion of democratic freedoms. A systematic effort to weaken or eliminate pro-democracy forces is most prevalent among authoritarian regimes in the former Soviet Union. But governments in Asia, Africa, the Middle East, and Latin America have also taken steps to diminish freedom of assembly, smother civil society, and silence critics.

Thus far, this campaign to stifle civil society and squeeze potential sources or pro-democracy activism has mainly played out in those societies already under dictatorial rule, such as Belarus and Uzbekistan, and those clearly moving in an authoritarian direction, such as Russia and Venezuela.

Arch Paddington,
"Freedom Stagnation Amid Pushback Against Democracy,"
Freedom in the World, 2007.
Accessed online at www.freedomhouse.org.

with a constitutional referendum that, among other things, would allow him unlimited reelections.

In Georgia, President Mikhail Saakshvili has come under strong Western criticism for imposing a state of emergency on Nov. 7 [2007] after police violently broke up a large protest gathering. The protests were sparked by opposition allegations of corruption and the possible involvement of Saakshvili's government in a murder plot.

Behind the bad news, say experts, are a number of factors. One is that the wave of democracy unleashed following the fall of the Berlin Wall has run its natural course. Those nations ripe for political change have experienced it and now are trying to consolidate their gains.

Another problem is that in some countries citizens are confronting what they feel are democracy's weaknesses. They have gained a vote, but remain dissatisfied with their lot.

"It's tough sledding for democracy right now," said Vin Weber, chairman of the National Endowment for Democracy, at a Sept. 12 [2007] Carnegie seminar.

The high price of oil is not helping. Non-democratic but petroleum-rich states such as Venezuela, Kazakhstan, Iran, Saudi Arabia, the United Arab Emirates, and Angola can use their flush coffers to placate their citizens, and help their neighbors.

"It gives them ready money to go out and promote their style of politics," says Mr. Carothers of Carnegie.

In addition, revelations about warrantless wiretapping, waterboarding, and other controversies related to Iraq and the war on terror have not helped the US image abroad. That gives antidemocrats ammunition to try and discredit the US style of government.

Russia and China

Then there are the examples of Russia and China. Both are doing well economically, though for different reasons. Both present themselves to the rest of the world as alternatives to what they charge is Western chaos.

"The narrative that Putin is using to explain his actions to his people is that he has brought order to Russia after the chaos that the US foisted on them after the collapse of the Soviet Union," says Thomas Melia of Freedom House.

Putin, as well as Chávez of Venezuela, and Hamas officials in the Palestinian Authority, deliver services to the lowest sectors of society in a manner that democracy did not seem able to do, according to US experts.

And while there may not yet be an Axis of Autocracy, Venezuela, Iran, Russia, China, and others press what they consider their advantages in as many international organizations and forums as they can.

"In the last year and a half [since early 2006], what you've seen is more effective coordination of autocracies, while democrats dither," says Mr. Melia.

Europe and the free nations of Latin and Central America need to understand there is a real problem, and join with the US to counter this propaganda, says Melia.

"There's another cold war underway," he says. "It's not East vs. West, but democracy versus nondemocracy."

*"Not surprisingly, young people feel ex-
cluded from the democratic process."*

Governments Should Lower
the Voting Age to Sixteen to
Expand Voting Rights

Kees Aarts and Charlotte van Hees

*The following viewpoint, written by Kees Aarts and Charlotte
van Hees, supports granting the vote to anyone age sixteen and
older. The authors examine the legal, political, and educational
arguments for expanding voting rights to youths and use both
scholarly research and contemporary examples to support the
benefits of youth voting. They also detail how youth voting can
contribute to strengthening democracy. Kees Aarts is a professor
at the University of Twente in the Netherlands, and Charlotte
van Hees works for the United Nations Youth Program in New
York.*

As you read, consider the following questions:

1. What article of the United Nations Convention on the
   Rights of the Child implies that youths have the right to
   participate in politics, according to the authors?

Kees Aarts and Charlotte van Hees, "Lowering the Voting Age: European Debates and
Experiences," *Electoral Insight*, vol. 5, July 2003, pp. 42–45. Reproduced by permission of the publisher and the authors. Accessed online at www.elections.ca/eca/eim/
article_search/article.asp?id=54&lang=e&frmPageSize=&textonly=false.

2. Is the voter turnout rate among young voters higher or lower than average, as mentioned in the viewpoint?

3. What European country does Aarts and van Hees say allows sixteen-year-olds to vote in elections in three states?

The motives of supporters and opponents of lowering the voting age are very similar in . . . various countries. Their arguments can roughly be divided into three categories: legal, political and educational.

Legal Arguments

Legally, young people come of age when they turn 18. Disregarding minor legal differences among the European countries, this means that 18-year-olds can be held fully responsible for their actions, can stand trial in an adult court, can marry without parental consent and can start their own businesses. This is an argument against voting at 16. The counterargument is that many other legal rights and duties are granted at 16, such as joining the military, buying alcohol, leaving school and paying taxes. Supporters of voting at 16 have highlighted these inconsistencies affecting young people's rights and responsibilities at different ages. In some of the German states, e.g., Lower Saxony, it was the decisive argument for lowering the voting age at the local level.

The right to participate is implicitly granted in Article 12 of the United Nations Convention on the Rights of the Child, which all Western European countries support. Article 12 states that the right to express views freely in all matters affecting the child is given to every child who is capable of forming his or her views, the views of the child being given due weight in accordance with his or her age and maturity. Although not literally a "right to participate" in matters affecting the child, it is often interpreted as such. Consequently, it can be argued that this treaty provides legal grounds for lowering the voting age.

Voting Ages Around the World					
Fifteen	**Sixteen**	**Seventeen**	**Eighteen**	**Twenty**	**Twenty-one***
Iran	Austria	East Timor	168 countries around the world, including the United States.	Cameroon	Central African Republic
	Brazil	Indonesia		Japan	Fiji
	Cuba	North Korea		South Korea	Gabon
	Nicaragua	Seychelles		Nauru	Kuwait
		Sudan		Taiwan	Lebanon
				Tunisia	Malaysia
					Maldives
					Monaco
					Morocco
					Oman
					Pakistan
					Samoa
					Singapore
					Solomon Islands
					Tokelau
* Uzbekistan grants the right to vote at twenty-five and in Italy citizens have to be twenty-five to vote in Senate elections.					Tonga

Political Arguments

Politicians and young people, it is often claimed, live in different worlds and speak different languages. Many politicians regard young people as objects of policy. Youth policies typically focus on the (relatively few) young people who show deviant behaviour. Not surprisingly, young people feel excluded from the democratic process.

It is argued that giving 16- and 17-year-olds the right to vote will provide political parties with an incentive to make politics more interesting, and to speak and write in language that young people understand. Skeptics hold that politicians create the wish for voting rights, rather than respond to it. Politicians are attracted by the advantages of a new potential electorate. It is true that the supporters of voting at 16 are mainly found among left-wing, green, and liberal parties, which in Europe have a relatively young electorate.

Educational Arguments

The two most frequently mentioned arguments against lowering the voting age are that it will have a negative effect on voter turnout, and that young people tend to vote for extremist parties. Both arguments build on the assumption that voting requires a civic maturity that is absent in the typical 16-year-old.

189

This reasoning has, however, also been reversed. The turn-out rate among young people has always been relatively low, but lately it has been suggested that turnout no longer rises as younger generations age. Young people are not attracted by election-related political activities, and increasing numbers remain uninterested when they grow older. [Researchers Antonio] Schizzerotto and [Giancarlo] Gasperoni describe this as a threat to democracy:

> Limited political participation—voting, membership in political parties, in youth associations and organizations, and representation in decision-making bodies—is understood as a major youth problem in most Western European countries.... The declining political engagement and traditional societal participation among youth is perceived as a threat to the future of the representative democracy....

Therefore, it is argued, youth must get involved in electoral politics at a younger age—and granting them the right to vote might help. Meanwhile, it is interesting that many young people, when asked in surveys for their opinion on lowering the voting age, oppose it. They believe that they lack the political knowledge to vote. However, their support increases when they are asked if they think lowering the voting age to 16 would be a good idea if their political knowledge were improved. In Britain, since September 2002, civic education has been part of the national curriculum for secondary schools. The "Votes at 16" campaign used the launch of this subject to support its case.

What about voting for extreme, anti-system parties? Research in three German states that have recently lowered the voting age from 18 to 16 shows that these new voters do vote in different patterns than older voters; however a uniform trend is absent. Electoral statistics from the 1999 local elections in North Rhine-Westphalia show that the Greens and the liberal FDP (Freie demokratische Partei) [Free Democratic Party] are more popular among young people, at the expense of the SPD [Social Democratic Party] and CDU (Christlich demokratische Union Deutschlands) [Christian Democratic Union of Germany]. But in the 1996 Lower Saxony local elections, surveys in the cities of Hannover and Braunschweig show that the CDU and Greens received more votes among the young. Finally, in the 1999 Saxony-Anhalt local elections, the differences in party preferences were hardly noticeable. It is important to note that in none of these states is there a strong tendency among the young to vote for parties of the extreme left or right.

Youth Voting

Traditionally, voting is regarded as a more or less purposeful vehicle for expressing political preferences, which is more easily used by those people who have the relevant resources (notably education) at their disposal.

Although its importance for the individual decision to vote or not is unquestioned, this resource-oriented explanation alone accounts for only a small fraction of the decision to vote or not (typically less than 10 percent). In the search for better explanations, one variable also appeared to be uniformly relevant. This is the age of the voter. Research suggests that people become more inclined to vote when they grow older, but that the relationship reverses for the elderly. In addition to this life-cycle effect of age, a generational explanation of turnout has also often been suggested: younger generations vote less than older generations, even when they grow older.

Recent publications have highlighted other age-related factors in the explanation of turnout. [Political scientist Eric] Plutzer (2002) presents and tests a "developmental theory of turnout", which emphasizes the habitual nature of voting and the crucial role of childhood socialization into voting. Whether first-time voters do actually cast a vote is, to a considerable extent, dependent on their parents' social and political re- sources; only later in life are these resources replaced by ac- quired habits.

This developmental approach to voting might fit well with the educational arguments for lowering the voting age that we referred to above. At age 16, most young persons still attend school. Civic education classes, which are commonly required before age 18, may support the socialization into voting hab- its—together with a competitive electoral contest.

The research in three German states on the turnout level of 16–18-year-olds lends some support to this hypothesis. In North Rhine-Westphalia, the turnout among 16–21-year-olds was slightly below the average for the whole electorate, but clearly higher—by about 5 to 8 percent—than among those aged 21–30. Similar results hold for Lower Saxony, where 16– 18-year-olds vote at a level comparable to 35–45-year-olds. Fi- nally, a similar conclusion can be drawn for the 1999 local elections in Saxony-Anhalt.

If the developmental theory of turnout holds, these gen- erations of 16–18-year-olds in Germany are more likely to ac- quire the habit of voting than their predecessors, who learned to vote only at age 18. This may be a good sign for the future of electoral democracy.

"Maturity is fundamental to the question of legal minimum ages."

Governments Should Not Lower the Voting Age to Sixteen to Expand Voting Rights

The Electoral Commission, United Kingdom

In the following viewpoint, the government agency in the United Kingdom (UK), the Electoral Commission, recommends against lowering the voting age to sixteen. The commission's recommendations are based on the argument that many young people are not mature enough to vote and that the country would need to implement much better civic education programs before the age could be lowered to sixteen. The Electoral Commission of the United Kingdom is an independent agency that was created by the British Parliament to oversee the country's campaigns and elections.

As you read, consider the following questions:

1. What is the voting age for most countries, according to the viewpoint?

United Kingdom Electoral Commission, *Age of Electoral Majority: Report and Recommendations*, London, UK: The Electoral Commission, 2004. Copyright © The Electoral Commission 2004. Reproduced by permission.

2. Does the public in the UK support or oppose lowering the voting age to sixteen, according to the author?

3. Does the Electoral Commission assert that lowering the voting age would increase or decrease turnout in elections?

There have been growing calls to reduce the minimum voting and/or candidacy age as a way of encouraging participation in representative democracy by young people. The Electoral Commission of the United Kingdom (UK) has undertaken this review over the last 12 months, partly in recognition of that trend, and partly in response to a specific request from young people that we 'seriously consider the arguments for lowering the voting age'.

Almost all countries have a minimum voting age of 18. The picture is less clear with candidacy, but most countries similar to the UK have the same minimum age for both voting and candidacy. The situation in other countries sets the context for the debate, but should not be the conclusive argument.

Minimum Age Limits and Maturity

Much has been made of other rights that apply at 16, for example, marriage, joining the armed forces, and liability to taxation, but the detail of some of these rights is often more complex than may appear (for example, the need to gain parental consent in order to exercise the right before age 18). Furthermore, the age at which rights and responsibilities accrue varies greatly and no other single right is directly comparable with the right to vote or stand at elections. In the absence of a wider debate about the general age of majority (which goes beyond the Commission's expertise and remit), each right should therefore be considered ultimately in its own context.

Maturity is fundamental to the question of legal minimum ages and the most important aspect of maturity in the

Voting and Taxation

Popular history remembers the slogan "No taxation without representation" from the time when the American colonies were resisting the tea tax imposed on them by the British Parliament. It was felt that representatives from the colonies should have a say in decisions that directly affected them.

The phrase "No taxation without representation" is now often heard in support of lowering the voting age. Many argue that, as many 16 year-olds are tax-payers, they should be able to vote for the people who set those taxes. However, others say that if we followed this argument to its logical conclusion we would give the vote to young children, as everybody pays taxes in one form or another (for example VAT [value-added tax] on sweets or video games).

Citizenship Foundation, "Voting Age: Reduction to 16,"
Teaching Controversial Subjects, 2006. Accessed online at
www.citizenshipfoundation.org.uk/main/page.php?77.

context of electoral rights seems to be the development of social awareness and responsibility. All that we have seen suggests that many young people under 18 would probably be ready to use the right to vote, but many others do not appear ready. Defining what is 'sufficiently mature' in relation to voting cannot be a precise test and must therefore rest to a large extent on the views of society as a whole. In this regard a wider national debate about the general age of majority would be helpful, as it has been over 35 years since the last formal review.

Citizenship Education

In the last few years there has been increasing focus on citizenship teaching in formal education, although the way it is taught varies across the UK. It is not just factual political literacy that is important—other aspects of citizenship education help young people understand 'politics' in the context of wider society and their own communities.

There is some logic in the argument that maintaining a gap between the end of compulsory citizenship education (at 16) and the right to exercise electoral rights may be counterproductive. But the strength of this argument depends on the quality of the citizenship education.

Independent assessment suggests citizenship education is still very much in its infancy. Accordingly, it is not sensible to found any recommendation about electoral rights on the current state of citizenship teaching in schools. However, the Commission strongly supports the principle of citizenship teaching, both during and beyond compulsory schooling. Furthermore, were the subject to develop more fully, this may change the context for the debate on electoral rights.

What Does the Public Think?

Most responses to our consultation supported a voting age of 16, but more general opinion polling suggests strong support for keeping the current minimum. Even young people themselves seem divided on whether they are ready to be given voting rights at 16. Public opinion also seems opposed to lowering the candidacy age, but views on this appear less strongly held.

The available evidence certainly suggests that lowering the voting age would decrease overall turnout in the short-term, and the longer-term effects are disputed. In any event, we believe that the minimum age for electoral participation should ultimately be determined on principles wider than the potential impact on election turnout.

Lowering the voting and/or candidacy age may help persuade younger people that politicians were treating their views more seriously. However, the fundamental issue for young people seems to be that their views are regarded as important and are considered properly by public policy-makers, not that the particular age at which they can vote or stand should be lowered.

All or Nothing?

A number of alternatives to wholesale change were suggested to us, including:

- different ages for different elections (e.g., voting at 16 for local elections and 18 for national elections);

- pilot schemes for the minimum ages; and

- allowing 16 and 17 year-olds to register to vote voluntarily.

At the current time, the Commission does not believe that any of these options would be appropriate, although in any future review we would like to explore in more detail the idea of different minimum ages for different elections.

Recommendations

There appears to be insufficient current justification for a change to the voting age at the present time.

The Electoral Commission therefore recommends that the minimum age for all levels of voting in public elections in the UK should remain at 18 years for the time being.

However, circumstances may change the context significantly over the next few years. In particular, citizenship teaching may improve the social awareness and responsibility of young people. There may also (perhaps partly in response to this) be a wider debate about the general age of majority that can better inform consideration of individual age-based rights. We propose further research on the social and political awareness of those around age 18 with a view to undertaking a further review of the minimum age for electoral participation in the future.

The Electoral Commission would therefore expect to undertake a further formal review of the minimum voting age within five to seven years of this report. We would encourage the Government to consider in the meantime initiating a wider review of the age of majority, given the length of time that has passed since the last one.

Different considerations apply in relation to candidacy. It is election to office (not candidacy) that gives an individual political power and responsibility. The candidate selection process of political parties and the public election process itself already provide the public with the means to prevent individuals they consider insufficiently mature from being elected. Accordingly, in the context of the current voting age of 18, there seems no reasonable argument why the candidacy age should not be harmonised with the voting age.

The Electoral Commission therefore recommends that the minimum age of candidacy be reduced to 18.

Periodical Bibliography

The following articles have been selected to supplement the diverse views presented in this chapter.

Paul Boutin	"Is E-Voting Safe?" *PC World*, June 2004.
Barbara Boxer	"The Count Every Vote Act of 2005," *Human Rights*, Spring 2005.
Claire Fox	"Folly of the 16-Year-Old Voter," *The Sunday Times* (United Kingdom), July 8, 2007.
Diane Frank	"E-Voting Policies Causing Glitches," *Federal Computer Week*, May 17, 2004.
Anna Kaplan	"Follow the Nonexistent Paper Trail: The Technological Advances in Electronic Voting Machines Raise Accountability Questions About Today's Democratic Process," *Humanist*, January/February 2005.
Jeremy Kirk	"Group Looks to Monitor E-voting in the U.K.," *Computerworld*, April 30, 2007.
Victor Landauro	"Should the Voting Age Be Lowered?" *Junior Scholastic*, October 27, 2003.
Dorothy Lepkowska	"Pupil Vote 'Bribe' Denied," *Times Educational Supplement*, June 11, 2004.
Steve Rodan	"Voting at 16 in the Isle of Man," *Parliamentarian*, 2007.
John R. Schmidt	"Can Outsiders Bring Democracy to Post-Conflict States?" *Orbis*, January 2008.
Nikki Schwab	"Teach Your Children How to Vote," *U.S. News & World Report*, December 31, 2007.
Laurence Whitehead	"The Challenge of Closely Fought Elections," *Journal of Democracy*, April 2007.
Thongchai Winichakul	"Toppling Democracy," *Journal of Contemporary Asia*, February 2008.

For Further Discussion

Chapter 1

1. Lukas Muntingh highlights the reasons that convicts should be allowed to vote, while John Fund argues against granting the right to those in prison. What are the main areas in which the authors disagree? Are there any points on which the two agree?

2. Based on the Sonia Lin viewpoint, what are the main arguments for expanding voting rights to immigrants? Does Phyllis Schlafly in her viewpoint effectively refute those assertions?

Chapter 2

1. Emily Keaney and Ben Rogers argue in favor of compulsory voting. They contend that it increases voter turnout and enhances the strength of democracy. Do they make a compelling case? Why or why not?

2. What reasons does Scott Bennett give for the continuing high voter participation in Australia in contrast to the declining figures in other countries? Are there lessons from Australia that could be implemented elsewhere?

3. John Samples and Patrick Basham are both employed at the conservative Cato Institute. Is there a bias in their contentions for mandatory voting or do they present both sides of the argument in a fair and balanced fashion?

Chapter 3

1. Leila Hessini argues that women have made strides in terms of political participation in the Arab world with the help of women's organizations, while Asef Bayat contends that women continue to face significant barriers, but have

made gains through personal empowerment. What are the main differences in the arguments of the two authors? Are there any similarities?

2. According to Kintto Lucas, Chilean women gained the right to vote in 1949, but have not exercised their right in traditional ways according to their gender. What are some of the ways Chilean women defy conventional female voting practices, according to Lucas?

3. What steps need to be taken to secure voting rights for women in Africa, according to Rachel Horner? What examples does Horner cite to support her argument?

Chapter 4

1. According to Kim Zetter, a number of problems exist with e-voting machines. What are the most serious problems, as described by Zetter? According to the author, what reasons do manufacturers of e-voting machines give for not taking quick action to correct the faults? Are the arguments persuasive?

2. Jendayi E. Frazer and Peter Grier explore the role governments play in promoting democracy, but come to very different conclusions over how well countries spread voting rights. What are the main differences in the arguments of the two authors? Which writer is more compelling?

3. What are the main arguments Kees Aarts and Charlotte van Hees use to advocate in favor of lowering the voting age? Do the authors offer enough evidence to support their assertions or are there flaws in their contentions?

Organizations to Contact

The editors have compiled the following list of organizations concerned with the issues debated in this book. The descriptions are derived from materials provided by the organizations. All have publications or information available for interested readers. The list was compiled on the date of publication of the present volume; the information provided here may change. Be aware that many organizations take several weeks or longer to respond to inquiries, so allow as much time as possible.

American National Election Studies (ANES)
Center for Political Studies, Ann Arbor, MI   48106-1248
(734) 764-5494 • fax: (734) 764-3341
e-mail: anes@electionstudies.org
Web site: www.electionstudies.org

ANES is a joint program of the University of Michigan and Stanford University that is also supported by the National Science Foundation. The mission of ANES is to educate the U.S. public about voting rights and election matters. ANES analyzes voting patterns and issues in the United States and prepares reports and studies for officials, the media, and the general public.

Australian Electoral Commission
PO Box 6172
   Australia
(02) 6271 4411 • fax: (02) 6271 4558
e-mail: info@aec.gov.au
Web site: www.aec.gov.au

The Australian Electoral Commission is an independent agency of the federal government that manages balloting at the national and local level. It handles voter registration and voter rights, including efforts to protect minorities and disadvantaged groups, such as the Aboriginal population. The commission oversees the country's mandatory voting system. It is also responsible for voter education and outreach programs. The organization provides a number of publications on compulsory voting and voter turnout.

Cato Institute
1000 Massachusetts Ave. NW, Washington, DC   20001
(202) 842-0200 • fax: (202) 842 3490
e-mail: pr@cato.org
Web site: www.cato.org

Founded in 1977 by Edward H. Crane, the Cato Institute is a nonprofit, research center that approaches policy issues from a libertarian perspective with an emphasis on limited government and individual responsibility. While it analyzes a wide range of issues, the institute has produced several studies and research projects on voting rights and the merits of compulsory voting. It has a large number of publications available through its Web site.

Center for Asia-Pacific Women in Politics (CAPWIP)
4227-4229 Tomas Claudio St.
Baclaran, Parañaque City   1700 Philippines
(63-2) 851 6934 • fax: (63-2) 852 2112
e-mail: onlinewomeninpolitics@capwip.org
Web site: www.capwip.org

CAPWIP is a nongovernmental, nonprofit organization dedicated to the expansion of women's issues, including the promotion of equal gender voting rights. CAPWIP is organized into five regional groups: Central Asia, East Asia, Pacific, Southeast Asia, and South Asia, and numerous national bodies. The organization sponsors research, conferences, and direct action to promote voting rights. The CAPWIP Web site contains reports, studies, and other information on women's voting issues.

Center for Equal Opportunity (CEO)
7700 Leesburg Pike, Suite 231, Falls Church, VA   22043
(703) 442-0066 • fax: (703) 442-0449
e-mail: Lchavez@ceousa.org
Web site: www.ceousa.org

CEO is a conservative research institute in the United States. The organization opposes the expansion of voting rights to immigrants until they become citizens. It produces several publications, including a compilation of news stories and items related to immigration and voting.

The Center for Information and Research on Civic Learning and Engagement (CIRCLE)
1112 Preinkert Hall, College Park, MD   20742
(301) 405-2790 • fax: (301) 314-1900
e-mail: akiesa@umd.edu
Web site: www.civicyouth.org

CIRCLE was founded in 2001 and concentrates on research of youth voting and civic engagement of those between the ages of fifteen and twenty-five. The center has an immense collection of information on youth voting available on its Web site and oversees a range of projects to foster citizenship practices among young people.

Elections Canada
257 Slater St., Ottawa, Ontario K1A 0M6 Canada
(800) 463-6868 • fax: (888) 524-1444
e-mail: info@elections.ca
Web site: www.elections.ca/home.asp

Elections Canada is a nonpartisan organization that was created to manage the country's voter registration and elections. It also conducts informational campaigns on voting rights and balloting. Elections Canada has sponsored a large number of studies and reports on compulsory voting and the nation's voting age. The organization's Web site has sections that focus on young voters and Aboriginal peoples, as well as voter turnout and the body's support for international voting rights programs.

Electoral Commission of the United Kingdom
Trevelyan House, London   SW1P 2HW
   UK
(020) 7271 0500 • fax (020) 7271 0505
e-mail: info@electoralcommission.org.uk
Web site: www.electoralcommission.org.uk

The Electoral Commission is an independent government body that oversees elections and electoral issues in the United Kingdom. The organization registers political parties, sets standards for candidates, oversees elections, and reports on campaign financing. It also educates the public about voting and political participation. The commission has prepared a series of reports and studies on expanding voting rights and compulsory voting in the United Kingdom.

Electronic Voting Architecture Research (EVA Research)
Damien Mac Namara, Limerick
   Ireland
(353) 61 208841
e-mail: damian.mcnamara@lit.ie
Web site: http://evaresearch.com/index.html

EVA Research was created in 2006 to enhance e-voting in Ireland. It is housed at the Limerick Institute of Technology and supported by funding from the Irish government. EVA Research focuses its analyses on transparency in e-voting and efforts to improve voting rights through greater accessibility at the ballot box. The organization's Web site features news and articles about e-voting, both in Ireland and around the world.

Immigrant Voting Project
Michele Wucker, New York, NY   10001
(212) 481-5005, ext. 536

e-mail: info@immigrantvoting.org
Web site: www.immigrantvoting.org

The Immigrant Voting Project is an organization dedicated to securing voting rights for immigrants in local elections. The project partners with similar groups in the United States and other countries to promote voting rights. In the United States, the project works closely with the New York Coalition to Expand Voting Rights. The project's Web site contains information on global trends in immigrant voting patterns, as well as individual country summaries, news, and a forum for interaction and debate.

Migration Policy Institute (MPI)
1400 16th St. NW, Suite 300, Washington, DC   20036
(202) 266-1940 • fax: (202) 266-1900
e-mail: source@migrationinformation.org
Web site: www.migrationinformation.org/about.cfm

The Migration Policy Institute is a nonpartisan, nonprofit research organization that examines issues of importance in the migration of people, including voting rights. The institute develops coalitions with other groups around the world to produce studies on individual countries and broad trends in immigration. The institute's Web site contains a variety of reports, including a number of publications on immigrant voting rights.

Project Vote Smart
One Common Ground, Philipsburg, MT   59858
(888) 868-3762
e-mail: comments@vote-smart.org
Web site: www.vote-smart.org/index.htm

Project Vote Smart is a nonprofit, nonpartisan organization that promotes voter participation and education in the United States. The project also maintains biographical information on candidates and comparisons between officials' voting records and their public stance on issues. The main goal of the organization is to expand voting rights as broadly as possible.

Public Affairs Center
578 16th B Main 3rd Cross, 3rd Block Koramangala
Bangalore 560 034 India
91-80-5520246/5525452 • fax: 91-80-5537260
e-mail: pacindia@vsnl.com
Web site: www.pacindia.org

Based in Bangalore, India, the Public Affairs Center is a non-profit organization that works to improve civic society. The center operates programs to improve voter education and increase access to the ballot box. The center also investigates corruption and political repression. The organization's Web site provides information on a variety of voting rights programs.

Voting Technology Research Center (VoTeR)
University of Connecticut, Storrs, CT   06269-2237
(860) 486-3698
e-mail: orlando@engr.uconn.edu
Web site: http://voter.engr.uconn.edu/voter/Welcome.html

VoTeR was created at the University of Connecticut to assist the state of Connecticut in transitioning to e-voting. VoTeR subsequently undertook a range of studies and projects to test the integrity of e-voting machines and supply recommendations on the effectiveness of the voting systems. VoTeR's Web site contains a series of downloadable reports on e-voting practices and machines, including descriptions of how current devices are vulnerable to hacking and fraud.

Bibliography of Books

Patricia Allard, Marc Mauer, and Jamie Fellner | *Regaining the Vote: An Assessment of Activity Relating to Felon Disenfranchisement Laws.* Darby, PA: Diane, 2001.

Douglas J. Amy | *Behind the Ballot Box: A Citizen's Guide to Voting Systems.* Westport, CT: Praeger, 2000.

Mabel Berezin and Martin A. Schain, eds. | *Europe Without Borders: Remapping Territory, Citizenship, and Identity in a Transnational Age.* Baltimore: Johns Hopkins University Press, 2003.

David Campbell | *Why We Vote: How Schools and Communities Shape Our Civic Life.* Princeton, NJ: Princeton University Press, 2006.

Susan J. Carroll, Richard Logan Fox, eds. | *Gender and Elections: Shaping the Future of American Politics.* New York: Cambridge University Press, 2006.

Congress of Local and Regional Authorities of Europe | *Women's Individual Voting Rights: A Democratic Requirement.* Strasbourg, France: Council of Europe, 2003.

Stephen C. Craig and Michael D. Martinez, eds. | *Ambivalence, Politics, and Public Policy.* New York: Palgrave, 2005.

Ann N. Crigler, Marion R. Just, and Edward J. McCaffery, eds. — *Rethinking the Vote: The Politics and Prospects of American Electoral Reform.* New York: Oxford University Press, 2002.

David Farrell — *Electoral Systems: A Comparative Introduction.* London: Palgrave, 2001.

Michael Fix, ed. — *Securing the Future: US Immigrant Integration Policy.* Washington, DC: Migration Policy Institute, 2007.

Marc Franklin — *Voter Turnout and the Dynamics of Electoral Competition in Established Democracies Since 1945.* Cambridge, UK: Cambridge University Press, 2004.

Dimitris Gritzalis, ed. — *Secure Electronic Voting.* New York: Springer, 2003.

Åke Grönlund — *Electronic Government: Design, Applications and Management.* Hershey, PA: Idea Group, 2002.

Axel Hadenius, ed. — *Democracy's Victory and Crisis.* Cambridge, UK: Cambridge University Press, 1997.

Ronald Hayduk — *Democracy for All: Restoring Immigrant Voting Rights in the U.S.* New York: Routledge, 2006.

Colin A. Hughes and Brian Costar — *Limiting Democracy: The Erosion of Voting Rights in Australia.* Sydney, AU: University of New South Wales Press, 2006.

Richard S. Katz   *Democracy and Elections.* New York: Oxford University Press, 1997.

Garrine P. Laney   *The Voting Rights Act of 1965: Historical Background and Current Issues.* New York: Novinka Books, 2003.

Lawrence LeDuc, Richard G, Niemi, and Pippa Norris, eds.   *Comparing Democracies 2: Challenges in the Study of Elections and Voting.* London: Sage, 2002.

Jeffrey Lesser, eds.   *Searching for Home Abroad: Japanese-Brazilians and Transnationalism.* Durham, NC: Duke University Press, 2003.

Brian D. Loader, ed.   *Young Citizens in the Digital Age: Political Engagement, Young People and New Media.* New York: Routledge, 2007.

Vivien Lowndes, Lawrence Pratchett, and Gerry Stoker   *Locality Matters: Making Participation Count in Local Politics.* London: IPPR, 2006.

Willem Maas   *Creating European Citizens.* Lanham, MD: Rowman & Littlefield, 2007.

Tatah Mentan   *Held Together by Pins: Liberal Democracy Under Siege in Africa.* Trenton, NJ: Africa World Press, 2007.

Ranjani K. Murthy and Lakshmi Sankaran   *Denial and Distress: Gender, Poverty, and Human Rights in Asia.* New York: Palgrave, 2003.

Fereshteh
Nouraie-Simone,
ed.

On Shifting Ground: Muslim Women in the Global Era. New York: Feminist Press at the City University of New York, 2005.

G. Orr

Australian Electoral Systems: How Well Do They Serve Political Equality? Canberra: Australian National University, 2004.

Charles Pattie,
Patrick Seyd, and
Paul Whiteley

Citizenship in Britain: Values, Participation and Democracy. Cambridge, UK: Cambridge University Press, 2004.

Rafael López
Pintor and Maria
Gratschew, eds.

Voter Turnout Since 1945: A Global Report. Stockholm, Sweden: International Institute for Democracy and Electoral Assistance, 2002.

Colin Railings

Local Participation: The Importance of Context. Plymouth, UK: University of Plymouth, 2002.

Dean Robbins
and Rob Grabow,
eds.

What We Think: Young Voters Speak Out. Bothell, WA: Book Publishers Network, 2004.

Irwin Shapiro

Democratic Justice. New Haven, CT: Yale University Press, 1999.

James A. Stimson

Tides of Consent: How Public Opinion Shapes American Politics. New York: Cambridge University Press, 2004.

Matthew J. Streb,
ed.

Law and Election Politics: The Rules of the Game. Boulder, CO: Lynne Rienner, 2005.

Carol M. Swain, ed.	*Debating Immigration.* New York: Cambridge University Press, 2007.
Alexander H. Trechsel and Fernando Mendez, eds.	*The European Union and E-Voting.* New York: Routledge, 2005.
Harald Waldrauch	*Electoral Rights for Foreign Nationals: A Comparative Overview of Regulations in 36 Countries.* Canberra, Australia: National Europe Center, 2003.
Robert P. Watson and Ann Gordon, eds.	*Anticipating Madam President.* Boulder, CO: Lynne Rienner, 2003.
Martin Wattenberg	*Is Voting for Young People? With a Postscript on Citizen Engagement.* New York: Pearson Youngman, 2006.

Index

A

Aarts, Kees, 187–192
Abraham, J., 70
Adivar, Halide Edip, 139, 141
African Union, 172
African Women's Development Fund, 149
Algerian Islamic Salvation Front, 104
Anthony, Susan B., 100
Apathy, in mandatory voting, 59
Arab women, gender equality for
  activism, 116–117
  bad-hijabi, 121
  discrimination, 116
  economic conditions, 118–121
  employment, 118
  head gear neglect, 121
  under Islamic regimes, 115–116, 121
  literacy rates, 117–118
  misogyny, 116
  NGOs, 119
  patriarchy, 114–115
  politics, 113, 121–122
  polygamy, 117
  post-Islamic feminists, 122
  poverty, 117
  public roles, 119
  religion, 114, 121–122
  sports, 120
  war/repression, 117–118
  women's movements, 114–115
Arab women, increased voting rights of
  defying taboos, 108–110
  democracy, 103

  education, 106
  electoral track record, 104
  family codes, 106
  female candidates, 103
  feminist perspectives/demands, 106
  gender equality/inequality, 104, 107–108
  global politics, 111–112
  inheritance rights, 107
  under Islamic fundamentalism, 102–106
  legal discrimination, 106–108
  media efforts, 108
  Morocco, 103, 105–106, 109–111
  patriarchy, 102
  political threats, 103–105
  polygamy, 107
  poverty, 111
  progress, 109
  religion, 105, 107
  resilience, 112
  school dropout rates, 111
  social/economic inequality, 111
  violence, 108–110
  women's studies, 106
Association Against the Discrimination of Women, 142–143
Association for Canadian Studies, 86
Association for the Development and Enhancement of Women (ADEW), 111
Atatürk, Mustafa, 138–142
Atatürk's Legacy to the Women of Turkey (Browning), 140
Australia, mandatory voting